About the Author

The author has a life-long passion for travel and an enthusiasm for storytelling. He was inspired to write his debut book in the hope that others will feel as passionately about travel as he does, and would then be motivated to follow their dreams and see more of the world.

Stuart has travelled in South America, South East Asia, Scandinavia and across Western, Central and Eastern Europe, though his favourite destination will always be the Scottish Highlands. In his spare time he tries to hold down a full-time position as a marketing director.

He lives in Edinburgh with his wife, Laura and their overindulged ragdoll cat, Hamish.

FROM THE BALTIC
TO THE BALKANS

*Tales from an Eastern
European rail adventure*

STUART MCMILLAN

Matador
9 Priory Business Park,
Wistow Road, Kibworth Beauchamp,
Leicestershire. LE8 0RX
Tel: 0116 279 2299
Email: books@troubador.co.uk
Web: www.troubador.co.uk/matador
Twitter: @matadorbooks

ISBN 978 1800464 575

British Library Cataloguing in Publication Data.
A catalogue record for this book is available from the British Library.

Printed and bound by CPI Group (UK) Ltd, Croydon, CR0 4YY
Typeset in 11pt Minion pro by Troubador Publishing Ltd, Leicester, UK

Matador is an imprint of Troubador Publishing Ltd

Cover illustration and design by Stephen Liddell

To Laura.

Home is wherever I'm with you.

xx

Contents

INTRODUCTION

M any people have asked me 'what first started your interest in travelling?'

I blame Michael Palin.

Perhaps blame is the wrong word. It is fairer to say that I *credit* Michael Palin. Credit him with instilling in me a desire to travel, to see the world. Watching his seminal voyage *Around the World in 80 Days*, made for the BBC in 1989, confirmed an urge in me that had been there since I was a child, that there was a whole world out there – vibrant, beautiful and exciting – and that I wanted to see as much of it as I could.

In actual fact, the seed had been planted many years before. Before I take you through the majesty of travelling from the Baltic down to the Balkans, through lands rich in beauty and history with stories of oppression and glorious rebirths to tell, let me explain where my motivation for such travel came from.

I remember voraciously devouring my dad's copy of *The Sunday Times* travel supplement each week, looking mainly at the pictures of faraway and exotic-looking places. Or exotic at least for an eight year-old boy from a small commuter town on the east coast of Scotland. I remember pictures of places like Positano in Italy with its inimitable positioning hanging off a cliff overlooking a shimmering blue sea. To me, these places seemed a world away yet at the same time both enticing and magical. It also felt to me that whenever I found somewhere I liked the look of, or wherever may have piqued my interest, my dad would have been there. To me, he seemed to have travelled everywhere. In fact, as I found out when I was older, he hadn't travelled *that* extensively outside Western Europe, and only once to the US – at the time of John F. Kennedy's funeral – but it appeared to me as an impressionable child as if he'd been everywhere. Formative years.

The other memory I have of this time is of the weekly ritual during dark, wet winters of sitting down with my mum and dad of an early Sunday evening and watching *Holiday*, the long-running travel review programme with its annoyingly catchy theme tune of 'Here Comes the Sun'. A bit like the BBC's film programme with Barry Norman, it followed a somewhat uninspiring sequential numbering system each successive year – though for some reason the film programme will forever in my head be *Film '84*. Now, in the late 1970s, there was no internet. No social media. No low-cost airlines and easy travel. When anyone wanted to plan their summer holiday, and if you were lucky enough to perhaps go abroad, then the main source of information was from programmes such as *Holiday* (hosted by the affable Cliff Michelmore) and its ITV equivalent *Wish You Were Here* with the seemingly perma-tanned Judith Chalmers. Each week, perhaps three different locations were selected and the lucky presenters reported back on the standard of hotels, availability of clean drinking water, what there was to do for children and any other number of useful consumer findings for anyone thinking of going on a package holiday to the likes of Benidorm. We would always watch it avidly for whenever there was a review of campsites in France, with my dad scribbling down information about Canvas Holidays and Brittany Ferries and which campsites were the easiest drives from the ferry ports. And indeed, two years running, my first initiation to foreign lands was under canvas in the huge campsites of the Vendée and Western Loire on the Atlantic sea-coast of France, magical places such as La Baule, the endless sands of St Jean de Monts or hidden gems like Piriac or Guérande. Thrilling adventures to an eight year-old, places that stayed with me and helped incubate the desire to see more of the world beyond my immediate shores.

My teenage years had seen school trips to Switzerland and an end-school/pre-university summer in Lanzarote, and for three years running from the age of 16 I'd harboured a yearning to spend my summer interrailing around Europe, the de rigueur holiday experience for people that age in the days before anyone knew what a 'gap year' was. But despite spending an entire summer holiday in Carrbridge with my family glued to a copy of a European rail timetable I'd found in the games room of the self-catering complex we were staying in, avidly plotting my itinerary as I envisaged criss-crossing Europe on overnight trains with my ruck-sack to sleep on, it never happened.

Throughout my twenties and early thirties, though I did get to satisfy my travel bug to an extent, it did tend to be more city breaks (Paris, Barcelona, Amsterdam, etc.) and traditional two-week summer holidays, albeit to superb places like Tuscany, the Neapolitan Riviera (including finally getting to visit Positano) or touring by car around Brittany, Normandy and revisiting my childhood in Western Loire. These were interspersed with a couple of longer-haul trips, once to New England and once to the magnificence of South Africa. So by my mid-thirties, though I had seen many beautiful places and been lucky enough to experience a lot more than many, the number of different countries I'd visited reached a mere twelve.

It wasn't until into my late thirties that my travel bug really took off in force. Primarily due to my life changing as a consequence of divorce. Finding myself alone, somewhat lost, unsure of what I was supposed to do next. The catalyst was probably my friend Alan. With Alan, it was almost a case of role reversal. During his twenties, he'd been young, free and single and spent a lot of his time heading off on exotic holidays – to Peru, to Vietnam, one weekend, I recall, to climb a mountain in Cameroon. We often joked that I was his unofficial travel adviser as we would regularly discuss where he planned to head off to next, and to an extent I lived his travels vicariously. So when roles reversed, with him happily married and me young (ok, youngish), free and single, it gave me the opportunity I'd yearned for since I was a little boy. He urged me to take this time as a chance to visit the places I'd always wanted to go. Specifically, I remember him saying to me 'Where's the one place in the world you've always wanted to visit?' Well, that was South America. So in late 2007, I flew 6,300 miles and ended up 22 hours later sitting with a beer in one hand and a bottle of water in the other, at 1 a.m. local time, in a little courtyard in a small hotel in the district of Miraflores in Lima, capital of Peru. My odyssey had begun.

Over the next few years, my travels took me not only around South America (twice, in fact) but all around South-East Asia, to Australia, to Scandinavia, to Russia, and to many of the places I'd had on a 'wish-list' for so long. At last count, my countries ticked off totalled forty-six and I have no plans to stop there.

In many ways, travel was a release for me. It took me away from a life that had gone a little 'off plan'. It gave me a purpose; gave me back my confidence; challenged me to overcome insecurities and fears. So I wanted to share that, in the hope that others who may feel similarly, that their life was perhaps passing them by, could take some inspiration from my experiences.

So, back to Michael Palin and why I wrote this book.

A few years ago, I watched the latest of his travel journeys, exploring the newly liberated lands of Eastern Europe. One city he visited stuck long in my memory. A city called Lviv in the former Soviet republic of Ukraine. I remember being struck not just by its beauty, but by the fact that this city, so resplendent with its rich history and blend of architectural styles, had been hidden away from the world for over seventy years under the shadow of Communism and the secrecy of the USSR. And now it was free again, relatively accessible, and irresistibly inviting.

So in the summer of 2013, when I was considering my options on where next to travel to, the city of Lviv came back into my head. One of the prime enablers of travel in recent years has been the deregulation of the air market within the EU and the subsequent rise of low-cost operators flying to all sorts of cities across Europe that were not previously served by the major carriers. Though they have their critics, the likes of EasyJet and Ryanair came as god-sends to people like me and opened up destinations that hitherto had not been so easily reachable (well, pre-Covid-19 certainly). I'd almost decided that I'd go to Lithuania, a country I'd not visited, but having been to Latvia and Estonia on a previous grand tour and loved the experience of visiting former Soviet satellite states rich in history and unspoilt beauty, I was keen to see it and had read good things about the capital city, Vilnius.

But Lviv kept popping into my head. Perhaps I was somewhat conscious – even subliminally – of its comparatively close proximity to Lithuania. Close enough, maybe, to suggest that an extended visit could take in both destinations? The more I thought about it, the more I wanted to explore the idea. And if I took in both, could I see yet more? I set about investigating just how much I could see, and how I could make it become a reality.

In this digital, ever smaller world, if you want to go somewhere you no longer need to wait until a Sunday night to watch a holiday review programme and hope your preferred destination is featured. Access to information and options are immediately at your fingertips. Looking at how I might travel across Eastern Europe, by train, two websites I found invaluable were the peerless seat61.com and also railbookers.com – the former for its unsurpassed information and advice around what routes to take and all aspects of travelling by rail in foreign lands, and the latter for its ability to help plug the gaps in booking routes and accommodation when the complexities of negotiating poorly translated Serbian rail sites proved just too onerous. *(On a side note: although East and West are no longer divided by an Iron Curtain, I will continue to use Eastern/Western here, as the sense of contrast and diverging histories across Europe remained ever-present throughout my journey.)*

And so, my next excursion was set. I would travel by train, from the Baltic Sea in the north to the Balkan coast in the south, weaving my way down through the old Eastern Europe, a journey of over 2,000 kilometres. And I loved every minute of it. From the baroque beauty of Vilnius in the north, through the golden domes of western Ukraine to the rich and complex history of Budapest, to the youthful vibrancy of Belgrade and the war-scarred aura of Bosnia, to the end point on the shimmering Adriatic coast at Dubrovnik.

This is a chronicle of that journey. Of the places I visited, the people I met, the history I learned and the cultures I absorbed.

I hope you'll enjoy it.

ONE

LITHUANIA

The journey begins

There wasn't any particular reason why Lithuania had originally come into my head as a possible destination. I do remember reading a great write-up of Vilnius, the capital city, in a Sunday supplement: 'Probably the greenest and prettiest of the Baltic cities' it boldly stated.

Having been to both Riga and Tallinn a few years previously, I felt that was a pretty powerful statement for the reviewer to have made. Riga, with its ferry port the gateway across the Baltic from Sweden, initially appeared imposingly Communist with its waterfront cranes and industrial appearance. But once off the ferry and, a very short walk later, in the heart of the Old Town, it beguiled me from the off, with its beautiful buildings, its parks and squares, the market stalls and innate friendliness of its inhabitants. That I stayed in a converted convent just added to the charm. The few days I was there coincided with a folk festival in the main square, featuring a diversity of musical talent from traditional choirs to a concert from an ex-Eurovision representative backed by the Latvian equivalent of Bananarama. And days later, after a bus journey across Estonia, the fairy-tale beauty of Tallinn, with its enchanting buildings and perfectly compact Old Town, looking out over the city walls to the Gulf of Finland, also left me with a sense of majesty.

So the reviews luring me to Lithuania had a lot to live up to, enticing me with the thought that it would be more than just the start of my journey from the Baltic to the Balkans.

KAUNAS

Although it was Vilnius that had initially attracted me to Lithuania, it was the country's second city of Kaunas that was my entry point for my journey south through the old Eastern Europe. Again, for no other reason than the fact that the low-cost airline I flew with took me there and I knew I could easily and relatively quickly get an onward train to the capital. But I wanted to see what Kaunas had to offer first.

A city of fewer than 300,000 inhabitants, Kaunas historically had the reputation for being the academic and cultural capital of Lithuania. I knew only of its sporting legacy, a rare 'talent' of mine being the ability to associate places across the globe with obscure footballing trivia from days gone by. Of absolutely no discernible use whatsoever to anyone else, admittedly, but it keeps me amused.

Kaunas airport was perfectly pleasant – on the small side, but modern and easily navigable. Onward travel options were not bountiful – bus (of the local, not shuttle, variety) or taxi being the two choices. The journey into the city is only around fifteen minutes, and allows the time to see the outskirts of the city and get a sense and 'feel' of the place as you get driven in.

I'd booked myself in to a modern-ish hotel in the east of the city, more the New Town than the Old Town which lay further west, beautifully situated at the confluence of the Nemunas and Neris rivers. The hotel sat near to the parks and sporting arenas of the city, and indeed there was a delegation of teams from a UEFA youth tournament residing at the hotel during my stay. All super-fit and energetic, whereas all I wanted to do was to get the air-conditioning turned up to the maximum setting.

Now, here is where I need to give you some context. And also to make a confession. I like to consider myself a relatively experienced traveller, and I am also – by nature – a highly organised person who will research and plan in advance. So my failure to consider the fact that this part of the world, at this time of year (July/August) might be extremely hot was, shall we say, 'an oversight'. And I mean hot. I did check, the week before admittedly, what the temperatures were likely to be on my voyage down through Eastern and Central Europe, though I was not necessarily expecting the answer the weather forecasts gave me. I think it was 38°C when I arrived (topping 100°F) and as I travelled further south and east over the course of my journey, it would rise as high as 44°C/111°F. It was unlikely I'd be joining the UEFA youth players in any form of vigorous activity.

Žaliakalnis and the church on the hill

Suitably refreshed, off I set, out into the heat to explore the fine city of Kaunas. And where better to start than high up on a hill, the best place to acquaint yourself in any new setting.

Dominating the skyline of the New Town is the gleaming white façades of the Church of the Resurrection, a huge modernist structure overlooking the city from the top of Žaliakalnis Hill. Although not a particularly taxing walk, I chose to take the funicular up the hill as it looked so quaint, accessed between a row of houses and elevating itself over the gardens of residences up the small hill. Though having just arrived in the country, the only money I had came straight from the ATM I'd utilised at the airport and therefore I had only larger denomination notes on me. The rather earnest-looking public official encased in his little ticket booth must have cursed me as I handed over the equivalent of a £20 note for a 2-minute journey that cost around 10p. Nevertheless, I consoled myself that it looked like I'd been his only customer of the day so far and sat down to enjoy the short trip to the top.

The Church of the Resurrection itself was huge. Huge and white. Huge, white and somewhat featureless, in fact. Surrounded by a concrete concourse, the views over the city were certainly impressive. Inside, I must admit it struck me more as functional than spectacular, hardly likely to rival Notre Dame or St Peter's Basilica. But it is more what it represents that is notable. I remember once being in Ghent, in Belgium, where my Australian companion was in awe of an otherwise unremarkable church that dated back to the 14th century. It struck me then, that to someone from a country where the oldest building is only 200-plus years old, that church would indeed have been remarkable. And so I thought about this modernist whitewashed church on a hill in Kaunas, otherwise looking like a bit of an eyesore, and realised how remarkable it must be to ordinary Lithuanians, deprived of their faith and places to worship for over 70 years under the atheist rule of the Communists and now free to build new churches and embrace their religious beliefs once more. It filled me full of optimism for the rest of my journey ahead, seeing how the people and cultures of countries suppressed for so long were embracing their relatively new-found liberty.

River walk to Aleksotas

From the concourse of the Church of the Resurrection, the city was laid out in front of me. I decided the best plan of action would be to walk along the river to the Old Town, and then back through the city streets themselves from the Old to the New Town later on.

The Nemunas River was, in all honesty, a bit featureless. The city on one side, the suburbs on the other, the river dissected by the kidney-shaped Nemunas Island in the middle. Home to the rather splendid Žalgiris Arena, with a 17,500 capacity the largest indoor arena in the Baltic, the island consisted of a pleasant green oasis with walkways and cycleways criss-crossing its length. Home also to a battalion of fishermen, patiently sat at the side of the river with their rods in the water, awaiting their hoped-for catch.

Crossing back onto the city-side at the end of the island, the rest of the walkway followed the river and screened the noise of the city roads by way of a large embankment, giving the walk a sense of tranquillity as I looked over to the southern bank and the greenery of the Aleksotas district beyond. As I came parallel to the Old Town, the impressive Vytautas the Great Bridge carried me in the other direction, south across the river. The main reason for so doing was to find the Aleksotas funicular, the second of the city's such modes of transport. This one transported me nearly 500 feet up the hill to the top where the best views of the city, and the Old Town in particular, were to be had. I love finding places like these, where you can sit and view the beauty beneath you, capturing the picture-postcard photo that the travel brochures try to show you, and reflecting on my journey so far. The views from Aleksotas most certainly did not disappoint, setting out the Gothic beauty of the Old Town resplendent with its white walls and red roofed buildings below.

The Old Town and castle

Kaunas Old Town – or *Senamiestis* – is hemmed in on three sides by a pincer-style confluence of the Nemunas and Neris rivers. Relatively small, the guide books will tell you it is a mix of Gothic and Renaissance-style architecture and the buildings are indeed beautiful. Pleasingly, the streets and squares are also relatively quiet and free from hordes of tourists and stag party revellers. Much of it is pedestrianised, making it easy to explore on foot and giving it a sedate, relaxed feel. Liberally bequeathed with churches, palaces and monasteries, it also has an air of cleanliness about it, the buildings either beautifully well-preserved or lovingly restored, all set off with a multitude of cobbled streets and lanes.

As I would find was common on my travels, at the heart of the Old Town lies the Town Hall Square (*Rotušės aikštė*), a beautiful open square surrounded on all four sides by coral-coloured houses and buildings with the gleaming white Town Hall impressively imposing at its centre. It is a charmingly beautiful square, not in any way touristy, even with the plethora of little cafés and bistros scattered around its edges. To add to the charm, a magnificent pillar, like an old lamp-post, sits on the square with dozens of bicycles attached to the stanchion like a bizarre funfair carousel.

The day I was there, it was filled with locals, families out on a Sunday afternoon to enjoy the sunshine. A small football skills centre was set up in the square too, a stream of young boys dribbling a ball around cones and honing their close control. A soft drinks vendor was running a promotion, handing out free cans to grateful recipients sweltering in the rising heat. It had the feel of a relaxed, safe and friendly gathering point, locals going about their business, visitors like me mingling unobtrusively. I really liked it. Kaunas was really growing on me.

In the north-west corner of the square lies the imposing *Kauno Kunigų Seminarija*, the Priest Seminary, the largest of its kind in Lithuania. And beyond the seminary is *Kauno pilis*, or Kaunas Castle.

The castle is not your typical castle. Not the standard fortress construction you would normally see, but instead a strange low-level elongated version more resembling a large dovecot with covered adjoining corridors. Surrounded by sunken grassy areas, which I took to be an old moat, the castle is estimated to date from the 14th century and sits at a strategic location overlooking the intersection of the two rivers. Well worth a look though, if only for its rather idiosyncratic appearance.

Heading back eastwards through the Town Hall Square takes you past the magnificent Gothic Cathedral of St Peter and St Paul. The cathedral stands at the western end of one of Kaunas' loveliest streets, the charmingly old-world *Vilniaus gatvė*, which meanders from the Town Hall Square back east to the New Town. Peppered with quiet little street cafes, bars and bistros, it is the type of place to sit outside with a cold drink and relax and watch as the world passes by on its business. Colourful flowerpots hang from the lampposts as people stroll or cycle along the cobbled lane, the tables busying as evening falls and dinner dates begin.

Back to the New Town

Dissected by an underpass, emerging onto *Vilniaus gatvė* on the other side marks the end of the Old Town and the start of *Naujamiestis*, the New Town. The main thoroughfare here is the 1.6 kilometre long *Laisvės alėja* which runs west-to-east in a straight line via a mainly pedestrianised boulevard. Albeit not one to necessarily worry the Champs-Élysées.

Comprised of shops of all varieties on both sides along the western end, it gradually opens out to include more bars and restaurants the further east you go, some of them quite trendy and popular, especially around the intersection with *S.Daukanto gatvė*, from where – incidentally – you can walk up to Unity Square (*Vienybės aikštė*) and see the stirring Freedom Monument and eternal flame on the Tomb of the Unknown Soldier.

At the far (eastern) end of *Laisvės alėja* lies the imposing Church of St Michael the Archangel, originally built as an Orthodox place of worship but which, after being subjugated under Soviet rule, was re-embodied as a Catholic church after independence in the early 1990s. With its Corinthian columns and cross-adorned domes, it sits as a commanding presence at the head of the boulevard, a reminder of the recent turbulent history of this city and country in general.

A peaceful stroll in the parks

My last sortie out into Kaunas the next day, before I departed on my long journey south, took me east of the New Town, to the tranquillity of the parks of Ramybė and Ąžuolynas. They comprise some 90 acres of walks, recreational areas and a large sporting complex, including the Darius and Girenas Stadium, home to Lithuanian football international matches and athletics events, as well as a multitude of sports halls and university sporting facilities.

My train wasn't due until lunchtime, and I wanted some quiet 'me time' to reflect on my trip to Kaunas, and the woods and trails of the park were perfect for such contemplation. Spotting squirrels scurrying amongst the leaves, observing people jogging the trails and watching others stroll about their daily business, I thought about how surprised I'd been by Kaunas, by its subtle charm and effortless engagement. What had started out as being a mundane gateway to bigger and better things had wooed me with riches of its own, and I commended myself on having taken the time to get to know a little of this unheralded city.

And so, the journey south began. Timetables had shown a regular service of trains between Kaunas and Vilnius, ninety minutes and just over 100 kilometres to the south-east. What I hadn't expected, when I wandered out to my quiet platform at Kaunas railway station, was how new and impressive the trains would be. Not all the train journeys on this trip would turn out to be so grand, but the train to Vilnius, a double-decker air-conditioned modern train that glided effortlessly towards the capital, was definitely towards the luxury end of the scale.

And so I sat back, watched the countryside fly past, and anticipated what delights Vilnius would have in store for me. The voyage through the old Eastern Europe was well and truly underway.

*Old Town from
Aleksotas Hill,
Kaunas*

*Town Hall
Square, Kaunas*

Kaunas Castle

In common with so many of the railway stations in Eastern Europe, my entry point to Vilnius was through the grandiose *Vilniaus geležinkelio stotis*, a pastel-coloured building handily located just to the south of the Old Town. And thankfully, within walking distance too, though in the heat I was grateful for the shaded areas formed by the overhanging trees that lined the streets opposite the large concourse in front of the central station.

In fact, that was one thing that struck me about Vilnius. It was surprisingly green and hadn't yielded to overly built-up urban sprawls or glass skyscrapers. A city of over 500,000, it appeared to me to be very much at ease with itself, content with its mix of historic buildings and sympathetically constructed new builds stretching gently outwards from the banks of the Neris River: north to the expanding modernisation of the business and commercial areas of Vilnius; south to the stunning beauty of the Old Town, classified as a UNESCO World Heritage Site, and rightly so too. It had an immediate beauty to it and, more so even than its Baltic neighbours of Riga and Tallinn, a particular romantic ambience. I liked it from the off.

A ten-minute walk from the station took me to the Gates of Dawn *(Aušros vartai)*, the medieval entry point through the city walls to the Old Town. Containing a chapel, it is an important point of pilgrimage for believers from Lithuania and neighbouring countries – Pope John Paul II visited soon after Lithuania gained its independence from the former USSR.

My hotel was five minutes further on, down the cobbled *Aušros vartai gatvė* with its low-rise white and pastel-coloured buildings reflecting the sunlight onto the narrow lanes of the Old Town. Situated on a beautiful little square opposite the Philharmonic Hall, the beauty and charm of Vilnius were immediately evident for all to see and I knew my few days here were going to be wonderfully relaxed.

A city of churches

One of the first things you notice in Vilnius is the beautiful architecture, an eclectic mix of Baroque, Gothic, Renaissance and Neo-Classical. Like Kaunas, so many of the buildings have been carefully restored and cleaned, giving the city an unblemished feel that belies its turbulent history of annexation by Poland then suppression by the Soviets.

It also isn't your usual Eastern European Old Town either. Fewer of the narrow streets and ability to wander off-map and get lost in the backstreets. Instead, it has more of a spacious feel to it where perhaps the buildings themselves define the character rather than the streets and narrow lanes.

The plethora of churches also emphasise the varied religious background of the city – predominantly Catholic, but also encompassing a large Orthodox presence and echoing a strong reminder of the city's significant Jewish heritage. The Cathedral of St Stanislaus and St Ladislaus probably takes most of the headlines, but there are some other beautiful churches and synagogues to be seen here – the Cathedral of the Theotokos, the Church of St Nicholas, the Church of St Theresa and St Catherine's Church are all located in the Old Town and all worth a visit, though there are many, many more to be discovered as you amble around the Old Town.

The heart of the Old Town

Vilnius Old Town covers quite a large area, on the eastern side of the southern bank of the River Neris (the New Town covers the western flank). Unlike many other Eastern European city

Old Towns, this one has more of a vibrant, everyday feel to it. Perhaps because so much of it is dominated by government buildings and a thriving university, it feels less of a tourist mecca and more of a dynamic, living, breathing entity.

Dominating the area next to the river and the castle complex is *Katedros aikštė* (Cathedral Square) where the majestic Cathedral of St Stanislaus and St Ladislaus is situated. Gleaming white, it is a stunningly impressive building, with its colonnade of six Doric pillars and a roof crowned by three magnificent statues. The vast Cathedral Square itself is a somewhat stark space, and tends to be used as a meeting place or focal point for parades, demonstrations or gatherings, though it is lined with seats under the trees to watch the world go past. In front of the cathedral, looking down Gediminas Avenue, is the curious belfry, a free-standing old clock and bell tower which looks more like a long-lost cousin of another tower in Pisa and which now acts as a well-loved rendezvous point for locals.

Moving south from the square leads you to the Presidential Palace, another wonderful building with an impressive history, having been variously used as a bishop's palace, an embassy and also allegedly where both Tsar Alexander I and Napoleon held court during the 1812 French invasion.

Across *Daukanto aikštė* takes you to the university which dominates a large chunk of the Old Town district. By far the largest and most prominent complex of buildings and courtyards in the area, the university has played a key role in the history of the city for over 400 years, though with an enforced break during the nineteenth century and then a Soviet-dictated conversion to teach mainly Marxist-Leninist dogma until independence was re-established in 1990.

A short hop from here takes you to the heart of the Old Town in Vilnius, to *Rotušes aikštė*, Town Hall Square, a

V-shaped plaza which acts as the traditional centre of trade and events in the city, including the annual hosting of the city's Christmas tree. The neoclassical, multi-columned Town Hall sits at one end with cafes and restaurants lining the sides, often with covered tables extending out onto the square. At night, this is a vibrant area with people dining out. In fact, on one of the nights I was there, I was inadvertently made to feel at home with waitresses from one of the little restaurants flitting around the al fresco tables dressed in tartan skirts. I'm sure it was for my benefit...

Just around the corner from the square lies *Vokiečių gatvė*, undoubtedly the busiest place for Vilnius nightlife, especially in summer, with bars and restaurants and outdoor eating areas aplenty. It was here I sat one night, comparing the behaviour of the younger generation to my own (and trying simultaneously not to feel too middle-aged and irrelevant). If, like me, you travel alone a lot you get used to sitting at tables on your own – if I'm indoors, I often have a book to bury myself in between courses or whilst I have a refreshing drink, but if I'm outdoors then the temptation of one of the joys of travel – people watching – is too much to avoid. And so, on this hot summer evening, I noticed the behaviour of two girls (possibly local students) at the table next to me. From sitting down, to ordering their drinks and meal, to the time they left an hour or so later, I don't think they said two words to each other. Instead, each sat enraptured by their mobile phone, thumbs frenetically moving across the keys as they interacted with absent friends or posted on social media. It did make me smile. There I was, hardly saying ten words a day out loud apart from the niceties surrounding any transactional interactions, and here were two friends sharing a night out yet choosing to communicate with a virtual world rather than with each other. *'Nowt as funny as folk'* as the saying goes!

One of the first things on my 'to see' list was to locate and visit a museum with a disturbing past. Formerly a courthouse, the grand but relatively innocuous looking building that sits on Gediminas Avenue across from the *Lukiškių aikštė* square became, after the Second World War, the headquarters in Lithuania of the KGB, the feared Soviet security service.

The building has now been turned into the Museum of Lithuanian Genocide Victims, and is well worth exploring, even if it's not an easy visit, telling the story of the decades of repression by the Communist USSR against Lithuania, including mass deportations of 'dissidents' to Siberia. The museum includes documentary video, pictorial and written material, plus the opportunity to see first-hand some of the more gruesome evidence, including various cells in the basement of the building where prisoner isolation was applied or where torture was practised and executions were carried out.

It is a chilling, yet valuable, reminder of the tyranny people on our continent had to endure until relatively recent times – the horrors that were being perpetrated inside this building were still occurring up until 1991.

Outside, on the walls of the building, rests a poignant reminder of the crimes committed with the names of many of those murdered inside inscribed onto the stone. For all that Vilnius is a superb, beautiful place, it is also sobering to recall such a recent and brutal history.

The boulevard and the river

The irony is that Lukiškės Square opposite is such a lovely open space. Where once stood a huge statue of Lenin, now exists a tree-lined park with paths that criss-cross the common and allow an eclectic mix of locals, tourists and lunching office-workers to sit on the grass or benches and enjoy their freedom.

Gedimino prospektas itself is a long, straight avenue stretching westwards from the squares and buildings of the Old Town. It is here, and on the roads off the boulevard, that you will find Vilnius's major shopping areas and a plethora of bars, cafes and eateries. All along its length, it is adjoined by a number of large squares. At its western end, at the bend of the Neris River, you will find *Nepriklausomybės aikštė* (Independence Square) and the Lithuanian parliament buildings. Continuing eastwards back towards the Old Town, you will also come across *Vinco Kudirkos aikštė* (Vincas Kudirka Square) which hosts, on the northern side, the Lithuanian government building, and just beyond that, both the Lithuanian National Opera and Ballet building and the Concert Hall.

A two-minute stroll further on takes you to the Neris River, which weaves its way through the centre of Vilnius in a meandering fashion. Here you can amble down to the riverside walkway that follows the river through the city and back eastwards towards the Old Town and the castle. It's from here that you can see how green the city is, even more strikingly so against the contrast of the white buildings and red roofs, with Gediminas Hill rising up from the embankment with the castle and tower resplendent on its summit.

The castle on Gediminas Hill

As with Kaunas, the castle in Vilnius isn't of your usual variety. It's not like Prague or Krakow or Bratislava with their walled fortress-like castles atop a hill. Vilnius Castle is much more refined, more a complex of buildings with the iconic Gediminas Tower at its heart.

The castle complex is really in two parts. The Lower Castle is more of a palace, with courtyards and museums and former arsenal buildings. The Upper Castle, a short walk up the cobbled paths to the summit (though there is the obligatory funicular for the very lazy!), consists of the three-storey Gothic Castle – Gediminas Tower. Views from here back over the city are superb, whether south to the Old Town, north across the river to the new business districts, west back down the winding river towards the New Town, or east to the Hill of the Three Crosses and to Kalnai Park. In every direction, there is a reminder of how beautiful a city Vilnius really is.

Within the tower is another museum, and one which I would recommend as highly as possible for any visitor to Vilnius to seek out. There are reconstructed models of the old castle complex and also stunning panoramic views from the observation tower, but it was the exhibition about the Baltic Chain that made my trip here so worthwhile.

I had only a vague recollection, from news footage of a quarter of a century before, of the phenomenon that was the Baltic Chain. Also known as the Baltic Way, it was a peaceful demonstration that took place on 23 August 1989 when nearly two million people across the Soviet-occupied Baltic states of Lithuania, Latvia and Estonia formed a human chain to hold hands across the 675 kilometres that stretched between Vilnius, Riga and Tallinn.

What struck me was the sheer magnitude of this protest. For two reasons. Firstly, in 1989 there was no internet, no social media, no way of easily making a message go viral and reaching the wider population. It had to be organised by word-of-mouth, by a gradual building of momentum from previous protests on this day in preceding years, protests known as 'Black Ribbon Day', demonstrations to mark the anniversary on 23 August of the Molotov-Ribbentrop Pact between the

Nazis and the Soviets which in 1939 effectively divided Eastern Europe into their respective spheres of influence and led to the Soviet occupation of the Baltic states. The protest movement's momentum grew throughout the 1980s, so much so that by 1989 it had reached critical mass and the idea formed for a human chain, with a route being mapped out across the three countries, buses being laid on for those without transport or for rural areas, and each district being allocated responsibility to make sure the chain was unbroken. The second reason for my awe was the bravery it took to undertake such a protest. Even in the period of glasnost and perestroika under Gorbachev, openly and publicly defying the Soviet Union in such an enormous way was a huge risk – the aforementioned KGB headquarters on Gediminas Avenue was, after all, still operational.

The exhibition shows photos and news footage of this momentous event, and it truly is a heart-warming and deeply emotive experience. Not only does news footage and aerial photography show a continuous, unbroken line of people stretching for nearly 700 kilometres, it recalls the protests that also took place in city squares with candles held aloft and spontaneous outbreaks of traditional national songs being sung. Less than seven months later, Lithuania became the first of the Soviet socialist republics to reclaim its independence and break free from half a century of Communist repression.

Images of such an enormous and visible demonstration against fifty years of Soviet occupation left me, I'm not afraid to say, in tears and reminded me that, despite the seeming helplessness of a situation, the human spirit is very, very difficult to break. That so many people, from three different countries, could come together and send such a message, is a lesson that will live with me for the rest of my days.

One final place I would recommend in Vilnius is the district of Užupis, the self-styled bohemian quarter of Vilnius. Meaning, literally, 'the other side of the river', Užupis is quite small but utterly charming, a Lithuanian version of Montmartre in Paris. Located to the east of the Old Town, accessed by crossing the trickling Vilnia River behind the Orthodox Cathedral of the Theotokos, it is a haven for artists, poets and musicians and has a charm all of its own, with its cobbled streets and gently-sloping hills.

Formerly a Jewish district, many of its inhabitants were killed during the Nazi occupation and the district fell into disrepair, frequented by prostitutes and the dispossessed for many years during the Soviet occupation. Despite being reintegrated with Vilnius following independence, it still retains a moderately run-down feel. In 1997, it actually declared itself a self-governing republic, and today hosts its own flag, currency and private army (of eleven men!!).

The district contains the Bernardine Cemetery, one of the oldest in the city and final resting place of several local luminaries. A favoured photo spot is at the statue of the bronze Užupis Angel, seen as a symbol of the district. I'd certainly recommend a couple of hours to wander around the district and soak up the history and atmosphere of this highly idiosyncratic part of town.

From here, you can also access both the low-lying *Kūdrų Parkas* and the steeper, wooded Hill Park *(Kalnų Parkas)* where you can walk up to see the monument of the Three Crosses, a symbol of the city that was built originally to commemorate martyred missionaries but now mainly to honour and remember the many Lithuanians deported to Siberia after the Second World War.

In the heart of a beautiful, green city rich with history and tragedy, this seemed like a fitting place to say my farewells. Despite its war-torn past, Vilnius struck me as not only friendly, relaxed and stunningly pretty, but (bizarrely, since I was here on my own) somewhat romantic too, and I took a mental note not only to sing its praises to others, but to return here one day and savour its delights again.

Lower Castle and Neris River, Vilnius

Old Town, Vilnius

*Cathedral of St Stanislaus
and St Ladislaus, Vilnius*

*Image of the Baltic Chain from 23 August 1989, when 2 million
people linked to form a 675 km long human chain in protest at the
continued Soviet occupation of Baltic lands.*

TWO

UKRAINE

And a short-cut via Moscow

Nobody likes getting up at 3.30 a.m. Especially not when they are on holiday. But my departure from Vilnius wasn't going to be of the leisurely and relaxed variety; instead I had an early morning flight on a Russian airline that I had never heard of and, I must admit, was slightly nervous about.

There may have been easier ways to get to Ukraine, but I had struggled to find them. My plan had always been to complete as much as I could of this epic voyage by train, to see as much of the old Eastern Europe as I could. But getting from Vilnius to Lviv was proving problematic. There were no direct trains. I could have got a train west to Warsaw, in Poland, and from there headed back east to Lviv. I would have preferred to find a train that took me south, through Belarus, and then onwards to Ukraine, but I'd not managed to unearth an easy option for that route. Belarus would have been great to visit – another country to tick off my list, given the likelihood that it was far from westernised, and probably still showed the relics of its Stalinist past. There was a bus I could potentially take, but as it would take the best part of two days out of my schedule, it wasn't really a viable option.

So I found an alternative solution. A Russian airline by the name of UTair flew a plane from Vilnius, via Moscow, to the city of Lviv in Ukraine. At nearly 2,000 kilometres to cover what could have been a straight-line journey of around a quarter of that, the detour would involve a 5.30 a.m. flight departure time and would without doubt be the longest short-cut I'd ever taken. So, with the alarm going off and the taxi idling outside, I made my way to the airport through the streets of Vilnius, deserted save for a few venerable revellers still straggling home from the previous night's partying.

Sitting on the small plane, with only a few businessmen on their red-eye commute for company, I couldn't help but contemplate the poor safety record of Russian airlines that disturbingly kept popping into my head. I thought also of the Innsbruck-bound plane that crashed in 1968 one week after my parents had been on the exact same flight. I remembered the Cuban plane I had taken from Havana to Santiago de Cuba crashing a year after I'd sat holding on to my broken chair back. I tried not to recall the Air France plane that crashed en route to Paris from Rio a year or so after I'd flown the same route. In fact, I just closed my eyes and thought happy thoughts and told myself to 'get a grip' while the plane rattled down the runway and onwards, to Moscow.

LVIV

Moscow's third airport, Vnukovo, apparently lies to the west of Moscow, but all I saw of it was the Flight Transfer sections as I quickly boarded my new plane and headed back south-west to Ukraine. My abiding memory of the approach into Lviv was the abundance of gold-domed churches gleaming in the morning sunshine, dotting the countryside of western Ukraine. I always remember being told at school that Ukraine was 'the breadbasket of Europe' and the flat, fertile plains I saw beneath me certainly suggested that this could indeed be true.

And so to Lviv. The catalyst behind my whole trip, the memory of Michael Palin's travel programme was still implanted in my mind. Bizarrely, as I was writing this book I dug out a copy of the *New Europe* series that covered his trip to Lviv and watched it again, for the first time in many years. I was somewhat astonished to discover that his report from the city wasn't exactly enticing – it was wet, bleak, the scenes focusing on the weather, the streets being dug up and the fact that there were stray dogs wandering around in the rain. That said, Mr Palin's commentary itself was warm and praised the fascinating history of the city, of its Western Europe inspired architecture and emphasised his firm belief that he'd love to return there. There had just been something about it that had lodged Lviv so firmly in my mind, and provoked such a strong desire in me to visit. And to make me feel so excited on landing to finally be in the city I'd envisaged experiencing for so many years.

A city of unparalleled history

Lviv is a difficult city to describe. Perhaps because it has such a diverse and complex history, having previously belonged to Austro-Hungary, Germany, Poland, Russia and now Ukraine. It would be forgiven for having a bit of an identity crisis as well, having had its name changed four times in the last century alone! Formerly known as Lemberg (when under German control), Lwów (Polish), and Lvov (Russian) the now Ukrainian city of Lviv is home to some three-quarters of a million residents and is the major city in Western Ukraine.

It was this almost unparalleled history that so intrigued me about the place. A city whose prosperity came from its position at the crossroads of Europe, a key trading post between the empires of Germany and Austro-Hungary to the west and the vast territories of Russia to the east. That is perhaps why it is so hard to categorise in terms of its look and feel, its architecture and culture. To me, it has more of a western European appearance to it, more Germanic or Habsburg than Russian. And as my taxi took me in to the heart of the city from the airport, the structure of the approach to the centre felt Parisian, with its Haussmann-style apartment buildings, elegant crescents and gardened squares. It struck me as the embodiment of a central European city, one which had flourished for so many centuries and then was forgotten about, hidden behind the Iron Curtain for so much of this century, only now being tentatively rediscovered.

Lviv has long been the intellectual and spiritual home of Ukrainian nationalism, which adds to the mysteriousness and charm of the place, and gives it an outlook that seems as much Western as it does Eastern. It was a stronghold of the Orange Revolution movement that swept across Ukraine in 2004, and again a key agitator against Russian/separatist politics which engulfed Ukraine in 2014, and resulted in the annexation of large parts of the east of the country to separatist militia purportedly backed by Russia.

My visit here, in the summer of 2013, was just before the unrest that swept through Ukraine with the Euromaidan movement in 2013-14. I subsequently watched on television as civil unrest reached Lviv, its large student population being the catalyst for protests in Freedom Square in favour of further integration with the West and the EU, and against increased ties with Russia. The situation, for travellers at least, does seem to have calmed down in the years since with Lviv generally being viewed as a safe place to visit again, but I'd always suggest that you check with your government websites (such as the UK's Foreign & Commonwealth Office) for official advice before you travel.

You wouldn't want to miss Lviv though, it's an absolute gem of a place!

The heart of Lviv

With its fairy-tale setting, coffee house tradition and UNESCO World Heritage protected Old Town, central Lviv was everything I had hoped it would be.

Ringed by churches of every denomination, populated by buildings with tiled roofs and an abundance of chimneys, Lviv has a diverse mix of architectural styles in keeping with its vivid and varied history. Further out there was some evidence of the functional Soviet style, but the centre remained free of such predictability and was a rich chocolate box of styles that made walking around such a pleasure.

To add to the city's rejection of the severe Soviet style you might have imagined to be at play here, the streets were interspersed with quirky little statues (such as an old man in bronze sat at a table, with a free seat across from him for you to join him) or indeed, when spied from on high, what looked to me like an old Trabant car perched on the roof of an apartment building. Upon investigation, I discovered it wasn't actually the East German Trabant, but an old Soviet era state-built car named a *Moskvich* (literally meaning 'a native of Moscow') which sat amongst the chimneys and formed part of a rooftop restaurant popular with locals and tourists alike. Not what I'd expected to find in Ukraine!

At the heart of Lviv lies *Ploshcha Rynok* (Rynok Square), the old market square which is dominated by the *ratusha*, or Town Hall, in the middle. From here, you can climb to the top for wonderful views out over the Old Town (including of the unusually parked *Moskvich*!), from where you can see the mix of architecture and abundance of churches laid out below. As someone whose first aim in any new town is always to get to its highest point, I'd definitely suggest this as something to do. It doesn't cost very much (my experience was that nothing really does in Lviv) though the hardest part is actually locating the ticket office, which was tucked away in an office on the fourth floor of the Town Hall. The climb is a bit of a slog, but definitely worth it for the vistas at the top.

Surrounding the square are a multitude of little shops, cafes, bars, bistros and a few outlets more tailored to tourists looking for fast food, all built into the ground floors of the former merchants' houses which rise from the square. The food in Lviv is varied. There are quite a few nice restaurants (some weird and wonderful themed ones as well), or – if, like me, you eat on your own and prefer to sit more with the locals and watch the world pass by – then there are a few little bistros with tables out onto the square serving more local food such as their *borsch* (soups with a profusion of things in them!), *deruny* (sort of potato pancakes, which are delicious), and *paska* (sweet pastries – Ukrainians don't go in for their desserts in quite the way we do!). The square is a busy thoroughfare, cobbled and mainly pedestrianised but with a tram line going down the length of it, so don't wander aimlessly looking up at the buildings on that side.

On its south-west corner sits the imposing Roman Catholic Cathedral of St Mary, or the Latin Cathedral as it is more commonly known, as ornate inside as it is impressive on the outside, just one of many beautiful churches within easy walking distance.

It is definitely a bustling centre, not a quaint tourist Old Town of narrow streets and relaxed tourist meandering. Rynok Square is the beating heart of the city, where life is still vibrant and the world has a purpose. Sitting having a coffee and watching Lviv go about its daily business, there was never a dull moment.

The centre of Lviv is not particularly big. It is not on the scale of, say, Budapest. You can walk around it quite easily in a day or so, which makes for a relaxing stay.

Surrounding the Old Town lies an abundance of sights well worth a visit. On the south-eastern edge of the Old Town you will find the Bernardine Monastery complex and the stunning Baroque interior of the Church of St Andrew. Across the road from this lies the Royal Arsenal, one of the few remaining parts of the old city wall fortifications. Beautifully preserved, you can imagine how the Old Town was protected by these walls, with their portals and loggias and gunpowder tower nearby. On the eastern edge, you pass St Michael's Church and Carmelite Monastery, the Church of the Assumption and the Church of the Dominicans with its magnificent dome. And just to the north of Rynok Square is the Armenian Cathedral with its little courtyard, and nearby, the Church of the Transfiguration. All of them are worth a quick look in, if only to see the ornate and often gold-adorned interiors.

Continuing the walk around the perimeter brings you to the magnificent Opera House, with its beautifully imposing façade and Corinthian columns rising to a roof crowned by three huge statues. It must also be the only opera house in the world to be built over a river – apparently, the River Poltva runs underground, beneath the stage, and down Freedom Avenue beyond.

With a large fountain in front of it, the Opera House is an impressive and imposing presence at the head of *Prospekt Svobody* (Freedom Avenue), the beautiful tree-lined arterial avenue which runs the length of the western edge of the Old Town. It's a wonderful place to visit, life flows as freely through the avenue as the old river surely used to. With shops and bars on one side, it's a lovely place to go for a stroll. Old men sit and

play chess, kids play with balloons, people sit and chat or eat
their lunch on the benches as vendors trade their wares and
romantic couples pay for pony and trap rides. Three-quarters
of the way down the avenue stands the huge and unusually
shaped monument to national hero, the poet Taras Shevchenko,
on a square parallel to Rynok Square. The avenue leads down
to its end point, at the impressive Mickiewicz Square with its
eponymous statue atop a commanding column marking the
southern end of the Old Town. The walk down Freedom Avenue
is a charming way to spend an afternoon, and I felt so at home
whilst here, the ambience and architecture being much more
reminiscent of a central European city than of far-away Ukraine.
I was liking Lviv every bit as much as I had hoped I would.

A walk to the High Castle

The next day, despite the unrelenting heat, I decided to explore
slightly further afield and take a walk up to *Zamkova Hora*, or
Castle Hill, the original site of the settlement that is now Lviv.
Situated north of the Old Town, it takes about half an hour to
walk from Town Hall Square. It's a fairly easy climb up, via back
roads then a set of steps up through the trees to the top. Though
you could go up the way I came down, through the winding
cobbled streets to the west, via the ubiquitous churches of St
Nicholas, St Mariya and the Benedictine Convent. Around here,
you could easily lose yourself in the narrow cobbled streets and
little squares, home to residential dwellings and the occasional
little café.

At the summit, once you get past the fact that it is dominated
by a huge communications pylon, the old *Vysoky Zamok* (High
Castle) is little more than a cobbled mound, dominated by a
huge Ukrainian flag. But it's not the ruined fort you come here
to see. It's the view.

Affording 360-degree views of the whole city and surrounding countryside, it's a magnificent place to come and experience. From here, you can see for miles and realise how flat Western Ukraine is, with the countryside stretching to the horizon all around. From here you can also see the remnants of the Soviet influence not evident in the centre of the city, the tell-tale vast swathes of uniform white concrete blocks of flats stretching out on the outskirts of town.

Being in places like this, when you are travelling (and especially when you are travelling alone) are great for contemplation. I sat and watched a train wind its way out from the city, out past the concrete jungle of ex-Communist flats and on its way eastwards, destination (to me) unknown. And I thought of how far from home this felt, and how vast the distance eastwards was, across the flat plains of Ukraine towards Russia and its almost infinite scope. And it reminded me of how far I still had to travel, southwards through the old Habsburg empire and down through the troubled Balkans and eventually to the coast. But for now, I was able to sit for a while and absorb the views and the tranquillity this superb setting afforded me.

A day in the park

I had a spare day in Lviv, as the train I was planning to take to Budapest was an overnight train. And I was glad of a few hours to rest, truth be known. Travelling is superb most of the time, exhilarating, constantly viewing new places and on the move to see the next. But every now and again, you cherish having a day to yourself, a day to do nothing other than chill and recharge the batteries for the route ahead. And I'd given myself just such a day in Lviv.

Generally, when I have such a day, I tend to take my book and head for a park. Partly as you can have some peace and quiet and enjoy the open spaces and natural habitat it bestows. But also, you can sit and just watch the world go by. People-watching (within limits obviously!) is a fantastic way to spend some time. *Where's that person going in such a hurry? Who's that lady waiting to meet? Why's that bloke looking so stressed? What are that old couple talking about?* Every person has a story. Every passing stride a purpose. You can really get a sense of a city, a nation even, from watching its people, what they do, where they go, how they interact. I find it a fascinating way to get an insight to the culture around me.

Lviv has quite a few parks to choose from, but I wandered south and west towards the university district, to the Ivan Franko Park, reputedly the oldest in the city. With a wide, long walkway stretching gradually uphill, flanked by benches on either side, and a plethora of winding paths through the trees to the interspersed open grassy areas, it reminded me a little of New York's Central Park, albeit much, much smaller. It's also within walking distance of both St George's Cathedral and the Potocki Palace, should you still have sightseeing yearnings to fulfil. All in all, this was the perfect place to sit and read my book and relax on my last day in Ukraine.

Night train to Budapest

I didn't quite know what to expect when I decided the best way of leaving Lviv and heading to Budapest was to get the overnight sleeper train. I've been on a few overnight trains on my travels, not all of them (actually, not *many* of them) hugely luxurious, especially when you are 6ft 6" tall. I remember taking the Reunification Express train from Hue in central Vietnam up to Hanoi, and drinking far too many cans of cheap Vietnamese lager with a seasoned fellow traveller from England I'd met on the train then retiring to my cabin which I found I shared with three Vietnamese farm workers. What would the sleeper train, which had started in Moscow and was heading for Belgrade, be like? I'd soon find out.

The first thing that did strike me as I made my way to Lviv's central railway station (which isn't central at all, by the way – it's way out to the west of town) was just how magnificent the exterior of the building was. If the Old Town of Lviv had survived Soviet-era architecture, then this edifice was everything you'd expect from a Communist-era railway station. Grand in scale, imposing, strangely beautiful, it was a classic monument to the workers' revolution, a throwback to the era of state-managed propaganda. I loved that it was still here, slightly battered around the edges maybe, but a glorious symbol of a different age.

As I stood on the platform with darkness falling, I reflected on my time in Ukraine and my long-awaited visit to Lviv. In some ways I was tremendously sad. Not just to be leaving, but also knowing that such a beautiful place had been hidden from the world for so many years, and now – with so much to offer – was struggling to release itself from the grip of those who continued to want to hold it back. It has been with deep sorrow that I have subsequently watched Ukraine almost tear itself apart, with one faction trying to forge new ties and re-establish old connections with Central Europe and the West and the other dragging it back eastwards towards a more isolationist existence.

I had waited many years to get to Lviv, and on stepping onto the train when it eventually pulled into the station (late, inevitably) I did wonder if I would ever get the opportunity to return to this enchanting place.

Town Hall, Rynok Square, in the heart of the Old Town, Lviv

Lviv Opera House

*Taras Shevchenko
Monument, Lviv*

*Latin Cathedral of Blessed
Virgin Mary, Lviv*

Lviv Old Town from High Castle Hill

A reminder of Lviv's old Soviet past

The majestic Central Station, Lviv

THREE

HUNGARY

At the crossroads of history

One of the staples of travelling is the joy of a long overnight train journey in some far-flung land. Invariably it leads to experiencing unusual situations, meeting colourful characters or dealing with something out of the ordinary. Rarely does the journey run smoothly. And so it was on my overnight trip from Ukraine down to the Hungarian capital of Budapest.

On boarding at Lviv, I sought out my cabin. Quite a simple task, so I thought. My ticket had a cabin and berth number clearly printed on it; I knew I was in the correct carriage; I knew this was the right train. Only the numbering system on the doors didn't match the tickets. Not an insurmountable problem, I thought, just find a guard and ask them. Though I quickly realised that standing in the narrow corridor wasn't an option – a combination of me (at 6ft 6") and my bag meant that no-one else could get past so I shuffled my way back to the carriage entrance and waited on a passing guard there. I didn't have to wait long, and in a combination of my pigeon-Ukrainian and his faltering English, we ascertained that my '7B' reservation number actually related to cabin 13. Obviously. He opened the door, pointed into the cabin with a 'yes, yes' and hurried off down the corridor about his business.

The only problem was, the two-berth cabin already had two people in it. One young girl, probably about sixteen or seventeen, who looked well and truly ensconced on her top bunk, and a young man, slumped on the bottom bunk (which I had thought was to be mine) who I must admit, did *not* look like he was necessarily as confident in his transient surroundings. The girl gave me a cursory glance and went back to her business; the guy looked at me a bit apprehensively, but didn't make any effort to move. Even when I weakly waved my reservation ticket at him and pointed to the number on the door, he just averted his eyes and pulled himself tighter up against the bunk. Right, where was that guard again?

Now, one of the things I always do on my travels is learn a dozen or so stock phrases in each language. My opinion, and it is only my opinion, is that if you go to someone else's country you should at least make an effort to communicate in their own language, and not expect them to be able to speak flawless English. The trouble was, my chosen stock phrases tended to be everyday communications ('Hello', 'Please', 'Thank you') or useful questions ('Where is…?', 'How much is…?') and a smattering of words essential to any traveller ('menu', 'beer', 'toilet'). I didn't readily have a phrase documented for 'I think someone is on my bed who shouldn't be and I'd like you to move him please'.

Undaunted, I went back out to the corridor and, unable to stand directly outside without blocking the passageway again, shuffled back to the end of the carriage and awaited the guard's return. When he breezed back into view, I had to improvise and quickly headed towards him as he was coming up the narrow corridor, blocking his path. Pointing to my ticket reservation and to the door, I cajoled him back to the cabin and opened the door, giving him my best 'can you see my problem?' expression. Thankfully, he seemed to grasp the situation without me needing to resort to the medium of interpretive dance to explain further, and the next thing I knew the young lad was being ushered from the cabin, not quite by the ear but not far off it. Having disposed of him, the guard returned and pointed to the lower bunk as if to say, 'there you go, all yours', and at that, was off again down the corridor. Clearly there was to be no maid service and changing of the crumpled sheets, so I smoothed them down and settled myself in to my shared cabin for the fourteen-hour train journey to Budapest.

Which brings me to my next dilemma. I've no problem with shared cabins, I have done that often enough on my travels. But sharing a cramped little cabin of two bunks and a wash-hand basis with a girl who looked about sixteen or seventeen? How were we supposed to get changed for the night? Did we just get undressed on our respective bunks, out of sight of each other? Should we just ignore the inappropriateness of it all and get changed regardless? Or should I just sleep in my clothes and avoid the whole awkward scenario? I decided to bottle out for a while, given that it was only 10 p.m. and sat on my bed to read my book as the train ambled and rolled along the tracks through the Carpathian Mountains on its journey south and west through the darkening night.

About midnight, the train started to slow, one of the scheduled stops obviously approaching. Our cabin door flew open and another girl of around the same age as my new companion started gabbing at full pace with Top Bunk Girl, and within an instant, my cabin-mate was down from the bunk above me and the two of them headed off along the corridor. Seizing my chance, I got changed and into my bunk, congratulating myself on my opportunism and I settled in to grab some rest as the steady rhythm of train over tracks soothed me to sleep.

It was about 2 a.m. that I woke up, aware that the train had stopped and then started again. Top Bunk Girl had not returned – did that mean I was to get the cabin to myself all the way to Budapest? Sadly, no. Within minutes, the door opened once more and Mr Guard appeared in the light of the corridor pointing cursorily towards the top-bunk, before stepping out of the way and letting an urbane younger man enter, who nodded courteously to me on his way to his berth for the night. Oh well, at least with the cabin full, there should be no further disruptions for the rest of the night.

Well, until 4 a.m. at least. The train eased to a halt again, and it soon became clear that this latest stop wasn't going to be either quick or quiet. Of course, I thought, the border crossing. Which meant border guards coming on, checking passports, going about their business. What might usually have been seen as an inconvenience quickly gave way to a realisation that this was one of the highlights of my whole *Baltic to the Balkans* journey. Something I had read about but forgotten until now. Because the reason for the great commotion outside, why there were so many people, so much noise and so much light was not just because we were at a border post. It was because of the ritual of changing the whole train from one set of wheels to another, a thrilling piece of mechanical engineering that – even at 4 a.m. – was a joy to behold.

At this lonely railway siding at Chop, on the Ukrainian border, the entire train, carriage by carriage, had to be converted from the broad gauge system employed by the old USSR to the narrower standard gauge system utilised by the countries of Western Europe. This involved each carriage being hoisted up by hydraulic jacks, the old bogies being moved to one side and the new bogies, with the narrower gauge, being slid underneath in their place. Once done, each carriage was lowered back down, secured in place and ready to roll off into Western Europe. It was fascinating to watch, standing at the door of the carriage as it was lifted a couple of meters into the air in the glare of the floodlights as one set of wheels was replaced with a new set before being gently lowered back down. This ingenious system, even for a train the length of this one, took under an hour to complete. Not that the reconstituted train got very far – before long we arrived at Záhony, on the Hungarian border, and the whole ritual of border guard patrols and passport examinations started up again in earnest. Well I did say that overnight rail travel in far-flung lands is seldom boring!

So at around 5 a.m., I must have drifted off to sleep, waking a few short hours later to the heat and sunshine of eastern Hungary streaming in through the carriage window. Soon we were snaking through the outskirts of the capital, the train looping around and crossing the Danube and entering the grandiose Keleti station in the heart of Budapest. I was now half-way through my journey from the Baltic in the north to the Balkans in the south, my voyage of discovery through Eastern Europe, and I was loving every mile and every minute of it.

BUDAPEST

The heatwave was showing no sign of abating. I'd thought I was perhaps getting used to it in Lviv, or maybe just the gentle breeze there had lulled me into a false sense of security, as when I emerged from the metro station at *Batthyány tér* (Batthyany Square), the temperature was even more blistering than it had been in Lithuania a week earlier. Undeterred, I made my way along *Bem rakpart*, the riverside promenade on the Buda side of the Danube with views over to the majestic parliament building on the other bank, to my hotel, where upon check-in I was once again indebted to the wonders of modern air conditioning systems.

Budapest is a superb city. Big and bold and beautiful. You can tell immediately that this is a city with an eminent past, the buildings here making an unmistakeable statement about the importance Budapest has in the annals of European history. It is also unlike so many of the places I'd been so far (and was still to visit) on my journey through Eastern Europe, being a modern, busy city rather than a quaint throwback to a different age of cobbled streets and old town squares. It had much more of a feeling of a solidly Central European city. It is unmistakably a city defined by grand imperial buildings, reminiscent in many ways of Paris or Vienna, an unambiguous reminder of the past dominance of the Habsburg Empire. I felt as if I'd hit a crossroads on my journey – turn back, or head south to the Balkans and I'd rediscover Eastern Europe; continue westwards and within no time I'd be in familiar cultural territory.

Cut in two by the majestic Danube river, the city is formed of two separate parts. The older town – Buda – sits hemmed on the western bank rising up to the Buda hills; the new town – Pest – sits on the flatter plain of the eastern bank, spreading and expanding outwards as the city grows. Most tourists flock first to the older, Buda side so I felt that that was a natural place for me to start too.

A trek up to Buda's Castle Hill

The best place to begin any city tour of Budapest is from Castle Hill, a long narrow elevated plateau overlooking the Danube and the newer Pest part of the city. As ever there is a funicular (after all, this is – despite first impressions – still Eastern Europe!) to transport weary tourists up the steep incline of Castle Hill to the World Heritage Site treasures at the top. You can also take a bus (cars are not allowed) or, as anyone sane would of course do in 40° C heat in the middle of the day, choose to walk up, through the narrow residential streets of the foothills and up to the magnificent vista at the top.

On reaching the summit, and having finished an entire bottle of water without feeling any cooling of my body temperature, I reached *Dísz t*ér (Parade Square) where there was a choice of directions. To the left lies the Royal Palace and gardens; to the right, the fairy-tale appearance of the Fishermen's Bastion and the Old Town behind. I decided to go right.

On first appearance, Fishermen's Bastion looks like medieval ramparts, but from some kind of children's enchanted storybook. Turrets, covered walkways, galleries and archways, all in a neo-Gothic style, sculpted from white stone, stretching 140 metres along the edge of Castle Hill. It is the best place in Budapest to take photos, affording superb views over the river, framing the huge, ornate parliament building on the opposite bank and the sprawl of the city beyond. The best place for photos, that is, if you can elbow your way through the throngs to find a spot. The bastion is inundated with tourists, although you can avoid some of them by paying a fee to walk along the top of the walls where the views are slightly less interrupted by the endless coach parties beneath.

Standing imposingly behind the bastion walls is the Church of Our Lady, or Matthias Church as it is more commonly known, with its huge spire and colourfully-tiled roof. The interior is breathtaking, with chapels and museums also accessible, though a fee is required. However, on a day as hot as this, it could be argued that the fee was well worth it to get some temporary respite in the shade.

Next door to Matthias Church is a somewhat controversial edifice, part of a multinational hotel chain. A weird mixture of a 1970s-built minimalist construct merged with the centuries-old monastery and Jesuit college, it provokes a mixed opinion amongst those who view it. To add to the sense of oddity, I was told that the only cars that are allowed up to the Old Town are those that serve this hotel. It wasn't my cup of tea, but each to their own. It wasn't a complete carbuncle, but not far off.

The Old Town in Budapest (or Buda, strictly speaking) isn't particularly big. A matter of a few streets to be honest. However, what it lacks in size it makes up for in colour, the facades along the cobbled streets being yellow and orange and terracotta. A walk along *Fortuna utca* (Fortuna Street) is especially pleasing, from Matthias Church at one end to the National Archives, Town Hall and Vienna Gate at the other. If you walk a couple of streets over you will find the delightful *Tóth Árpád Setany* promenade which offers fabulous views westwards out across the expanse of Vérmező Park to the Buda Hills beyond. The whole circuit won't take much longer than a lazy couple of hours but it is a lovely part of the city and surprisingly quiet (maybe all the coach parties are still fighting for prime photo spots at Fishermen's Bastion).

Heading back to Parade Square, you can then take the other route atop Castle Hill, south towards the Royal Palace compound. The palace, which is impressively illuminated at night, dominates the skyline on this side of the river and is up there with anything you will find in the grandeur of neighbouring Vienna. The complex itself is extensive, accommodating not only the palace and gardens but the National Gallery and Museum of Contemporary Art too. From the statued courtyard in front of the palace, the views over the river are exquisite, with a particularly good view of the iconic Chain Bridge. And the sea of Hungarian national flags draped from a row of flagpoles which adorn *Szent György utca* (St George Square) within the compound are a sight to behold. You really get a sense of what a powerhouse of a nation this was during the Habsburg era, and what a proud country it remains to this day.

You can also walk around the walls to the *Deli Rondella* at the peak of the bastion, the fortifications coming together like the bow of a ship. From there you can walk down to the green grounds of the Kemal Atatürk Park below, which affords a reprieve from both the crowds and the heat, as well as being a nice place to sit and relax.

Continuing south down the river from Castle Hill then up through the wooded slopes takes you to Gellert Hill and the Citadel at the top. The trek on foot (no funicular here!) is somewhat arduous, though ultimately rewarding. The views from here are glorious – not only over the Danube and to the new town beyond, but also back up towards Castle Hill, to the Royal Palace and Old Town beyond. The imposing *Szabadság szobor* (Liberation Monument) is a remnant from Soviet times, commemorating the loss of Russian lives to the Germans during the Second World War. It is a controversial memorial, seemingly loathed by the locals as a symbol of past occupation, but recognised now in a practical sense as being too much of a city landmark to tear down. Once again, it is a potent symbol of the complex history of this proud country and a reminder of Hungary's role at the crossroads of history.

Across the Chain Bridge to Pest

Of the many bridges that cross the Danube linking Buda on one side to Pest on the other, the most iconic is *Széchenyi Lanchid*, more commonly known as the Chain Bridge. It is to Budapest what the Brooklyn Bridge is to New York or the Golden Gate to San Francisco, a stunning twin-arched suspension bridge flanked at both ends by two enormous lion statues. Designed by an Englishman and constructed by a Scottish engineer named Adam Clark, the square at the Buda end of the bridge is still named after the latter *(Ádám tér)*. It makes for a lovely walk, high above the river and with the striking architectural heritage on both banks laid out in front of you. Catch it at night too when it is floodlit for a sensational spectacle.

On the new town (Pest) side, the bridge leads you directly to *Széchenyi István tér* (Szechenyi Square), with the art nouveau splendour of the Gresham Palace Hotel immediately facing you. To the left of the square sits the equally magnificent Hungarian Academy of Sciences Museum, though the square itself is not much more than a glorified roundabout as the traffic throngs around the on and off ramps to the bridge. Where Buda on the west bank was stately and palatial, the more modern Pest is busy, bustling and businesslike, though not without its own architectural treasures and beauty.

Continuing left, following the river northwards leads you to the *Országház*, the Hungarian Houses of Parliament, a building so stunning it dominates not only the east bank of the Danube but almost every single picture postcard of Budapest. Reputedly the largest building in Hungary, the domed neo-Gothic structure is reminiscent of the UK's Houses of Parliament at Westminster, though to me even more impressive, especially at night when the floodlighting creates an ambience of stunning magnitude. Flanked by the river on one side and on the other three sides by public squares, this is a breathtaking place to spend some time. The main square *(Kossuth Lajos tér)* has been undergoing a major reconstruction and is a site of national interest – the memorial at the north end commemorates the hundreds of protestors who died here in a massacre on 'Black Thursday' during the 1956 uprising. It was also here, 33 years later, that protests against the crumbling Soviet empire took place with an estimated 100,000 people in the square.

Adjacent to the square you will find the little square of *Vertanúk tere*, where the statue of Imre Nagy stands on a little bridge gazing over Kossuth Square and the parliament. Nagy, prime minister at the time of the crushed Hungarian Revolution in 1956, was tried and executed two years later and buried in an unmarked grave. Reburied in 1989 as a hero, his image stands today overlooking the new democratic centre of a country that has emerged from years of occupation, a reminder of a bloody and repressive history on our continent.

Cutting through behind the monument to Nagy brings you to the *Szabadság tér* (Liberty Square), an impressive and ornate public square, home to – amongst others – the National Bank of Hungary and the US Embassy. At its centre sits the Soviet Army memorial, paying tribute to the Russian army who liberated Hungary from the Nazis. As ever in Hungary though, with its turbulent past, this has controversial associations and is frequently the subject of fierce debate.

Leaving the beauty of Liberty Square and continuing southeast for a few minutes brings you to the magnificent Basilica of St Stephen with its striking dome dominating the skyline. Best viewed from the west façade-facing square *(Szent István tér)* you can jostle with tourists for the best photo opportunity of this exquisitely beautiful building. Inside, 364 steps will take you to the dome's observation deck for stunning panoramic views over the city. Or for the less energetic, a lift will perform the same function. Either way, the result is well worth the token fee to do so.

A walk up Andrassy Avenue

Inspired by the Champs-Élysées in Paris, the 2.5 kilometre long *Andrássy út* is undoubtedly a jewel in the crown of Budapest. Listed as a World Heritage site, this wide, tree-lined boulevard connects the start of the New Town by the Danube with the vast city park to the east. It has been variously known as People's Republic Street, Avenue of Hungarian Youth and even – much to the locals' disgust – Stalin Street, but in 1989 it reverted back to its original name of Andrassy Avenue.

I started at the bottom end, nearest the river. It is actually diagonally across the road from St Stephen's Basilica so not hard to find. I knew the park, and the thermal baths, lay at the other end which gave me enough motivation to walk the entire length in this blistering heat knowing that shade and water awaited me at the other end.

Andrassy Avenue can be seen to be split into two distinct parts. The lower part is full of bars, restaurants, theatres and luxury boutiques. The upper part, on the other side of the *Oktogon* intersection, widens out even further and is dominated more by larger residential buildings and foreign embassies.

I headed first to *Magyar Állami Operaház*, the Hungarian State Opera House, the most iconic building on the avenue, which was apparently modelled on its counterpart in Vienna. Inside, the marble columns and staircase vie with a mural-covered vaulted ceiling for your attention. You can take a guided tour should you so wish, or if you are lucky regarding availability, purchase tickets for a performance. Being on my own, I passed on that option and made do with staring in awe at the opulence within.

A little further up brings you to *Nagymező utca*, Budapest's equivalent of Broadway with its plentiful supply of theatres, and a block or so further on still leads you to *Liszt Ferenc tér*, a lovely side street lined with restaurants, cafes and bars and encompassing plenty of green shady areas to enjoy a quiet break. The food in Budapest is, as you would expect from a large, modern capital city, a lot more cosmopolitan than you are likely to find in the rest of the country, and a far cry from the carb-dominated dumpling and potato staples of the Soviet era. That's not to say that you cannot still pick up a wonderful goulash or Hungarian sausages (*kolbász*) and *csülök* (roasted piglet), but there are as many pasta and (Western) European menus available as there are traditional Hungarian. Whilst the Hungarians do not seem to be as attached to their beers as many – though the pint or two of *Dreher* I had hit the spot in the ferocious heat – they do take pride in their wines, with their *Tokaji* being the most well-renowned. And if you are feeling really brave, try the *Palink*á, a traditional fruit brandy that the locals seem to consume on all occasions and at any time of the day!

A reminder from history

No.60 Andrassy Avenue was once the most feared address in Budapest. To be honest, it is difficult to contemplate how one building could signify such abject horror, with different 'owners', for such a long period of time. The nondescript building (though it is adorned now by a striking black steel roof structure with the Hungarian word for 'Terror' cut out of it) was once the Hungarian headquarters of the Nazis – under the guise of the national-socialist Hungarian Arrow Cross Party – and after the war it became home to the *AVH*, the Soviet-backed Hungarian State Police, essentially an appendage of the fearsome KGB. Under both regimes, it was not an address you wanted to be taken to. There was generally little chance of you coming back out. The building is now a museum, the chillingly named House of Terror, focusing on the crimes and atrocities committed by both fascist and Stalinist regimes. It was one place – as a history buff – that I had to visit.

The internal exhibitions themselves are highly impressive, a mixture of multimedia effects, video and photographic archive footage and emotive sound and light. The props are unsettling too – a full-size tank, a mock courtroom and most chillingly of all, an all too realistic experience as the lift slowly takes you to the basement where the tortures and executions were conducted. In the lift, you hear the voice of a guard recounting dispassionately his job of taking prisoners to their deaths, and the sights and sounds of the prisoners' last walks hit you all the more when the doors open and you see the self-same corridors and execution chambers your senses have just experienced. It is no place for the faint-hearted, and some of the emotional delivery isn't exactly subtle, but it is brilliantly delivered.

Disturbing as the museum is, it does also raise a few questions around the issue of culpability. You get the impression very firmly from the museum story that this horrendous history was the result of occupying forces and the repression of the indigenous citizens, both by the Nazis and then by the Soviets, but there is just enough room left to allow an element of questioning around the extent of collaboration and how much the tyranny of both regimes was embraced by some of the natives themselves.

That notwithstanding, it is almost inconceivable to think about how one nation, one group of people, could go from suffering under fascism and Nazi occupation, tyranny and atrocities to then be apparently liberated only to fall straight into an even worse period of repression, torture and brutality by a totalitarian state apparatus under Communism for the next forty years. And to have both regimes sequentially base their oppressors at the same headquarters is beyond parody. It is not a 'fun' way to spend an afternoon, but one that is deeply thought-provoking and highly instructive and there is no doubting that the museum's uncompromising approach leaves a profound impression.

A dip in the baths!

Standing back outside on the pavement in the heat of the afternoon sun, my senses were still trying to process the horrors I'd seen and read about within. Where do you go after that?

The one place that seemed most appropriate was to continue to walk up Andrassy Avenue to its end-point, the vast open space of Heroes Square *(Hősök tere)*. The largest and most symbolic square in Budapest, it is a focal point for Hungarian nationalist expression and has been the setting for political demonstrations, notably when an estimated 250,000 people gathered in 1989 to honour the reburial of Imre Nagy. The cenotaph that lies in the middle of the square is inscribed with a dedication: 'To the memory of the heroes who gave their lives for the freedom of our people and our national independence.' Somehow, after the Terror Museum had revealed such a dark part of Hungarian history, this seemed perfectly apt.

The square itself is flanked by two impressive buildings – on the left, *Műcsarnok* (Museum of Fine Arts), on the right, *Kunsthalle*, the Hall of Art. At the centre of the square, behind the cenotaph, stands the mighty Millennium Monument and behind that, an impressive semi-circular colonnade of statues depicting important figures from Hungary's past. The vast political demonstrations that used to take place in the square have now largely given way to tourists with cameras and local youngsters on skateboards. Which, to be honest, is no bad thing.

For a slight detour, if you pop behind the Palace of Art you will find what is reputed to be the world's largest hourglass, erected in 2004 to mark the entry of Hungary into the European Union. Impressive as it is, don't sit and watch the sand filter through expecting an hour to pass as it actually takes a year to complete the cycle, before starting again each New Year's Eve. Oh, and when it was installed it seemingly replaced a huge statue of Lenin, which again brings home to you the journey Hungary – as with so many of the countries I passed through in Eastern Europe – has travelled on during its turbulent past.

Behind the square lies the huge green expanse of *Varosliget*, or City Park, where you are free to stroll, picnic, hire bikes, boats and pedalos, or visit the museums or zoo contained within. It's a lovely space to relax for a while, as although Budapest is not particularly hilly, it is still a big city and the walk up Andrassy Avenue from the centre to the park is long, especially on a day as hot as this was (though you can cheat and get the Metro back). So it's good to get some time to sit in the shade, to chill and watch the world pass by.

The main reason I'd come here though was to experience a staple of Budapest life. For in the grounds of the City Park lie the Széchenyi Baths, one of the city's famous medicinal bath complexes. Comprising a dozen or more thermal baths and swimming pools, indoor and out, it is a brilliant place to go to cool off, relax and soak up the local culture. You can spot the domes of the complex from just about anywhere in the park, the bright yellow walls of the pavilions shimmering in the sun.

You can rent a swimming costume if you don't want to have to carry your kit around with you all day. And modesty is still alive in this part of the world – with all the facilities being open to all, there is no going *au naturel* here. Unlike a sauna I once found myself in in Berlin, where – unknown to me – it was obviously *de rigueur* not to wear any swimwear, as I quickly found out when Berliners of all ages and sizes wandered in with bits swinging as nature intended! Not here however, thankfully, though the Budapesters do seem to take their saunas very seriously and pile in to the wooden benched enclosures in great numbers and with an earnestness of spirit which has to be admired.

Although there are numerous smaller thermal spas, baths and saunas to sample, the best experience is in the main open-air pool where the water is kept heated to a nice-and-toasty 27°C temperature and the thermal waters bubble around you. The most popular pastime here is to watch the groups of chess players, standing chest-deep in the rising steam of the thermal pools playing chess on boards laid out on the many small jetties that protrude into the pool. It really is a bizarre, but thoroughly unforgettable, experience.

Mementos from the past

My last outing in Budapest was indeed a step back in history. Situated on what could charitably be called a nondescript walled-in piece of waste ground to the south-west of the city, Memento Park is a graveyard for former Communist-era statues that no longer have a home. It is a brilliant museum, basic but poignant in its simplicity, with huge propaganda statues standing now in a wreckers yard, unloved, unseen and with only a procession of tourists arriving daily by bus to gaze upon what for a generation came to symbolise the might of the Soviet empire across Eastern Europe.

There are statues of Lenin, Marx, Engels; sculptures depicting Red Army soldiers in battle; of workers in the fields or factories toiling for the Motherland; icons from a different era. Where once these statues stood intimidatingly in central Budapest, atop Gellert Hill, outside government buildings, they now rest forlorn and forsaken in a field on the periphery of the city. It was in many ways a fitting end to my time in Hungary, a nation at the heart of Europe but for so often at the crossroads of its history.

*Royal Palace,
Castle Hill,
Budapest*

*Fishermen's
Bastion, Castle
Hill, Budapest*

*Chain Bridge
over the Danube
(with the
Parliament
building behind),
Budapest*

Statue of Imre Nagy overlooking parliament, Budapest

House of Terror, 60 Andrássy út, Budapest

Memento Park, Budapest

Old Town, Castle Hill, Budapest

Széchenyi Baths, Budapest

Heroes Square, Budapest

FOUR

SERBIA

Into the Balkans – in the dark

I departed Budapest as I had arrived – via train, from Keleti station. Train EC273 to Belgrade was scheduled to take around eight hours, so I settled back in my seat, some provisions bought, and looked forward to the near 400 kilometre journey south through the national parks and farmlands of the Great Plain and on towards the next leg of my journey, into the Balkans for the first time, to Serbia.

If the trains in Lithuania had been spacious and modern, then the same procurement practices had not yet reached the Budapest–Belgrade route. The rolling-stock was, shall we say, 'nostalgic' but as the carriage was quiet, I had my choice of seat and an unrestricted window view to observe the changes in countryside as we rolled southwards.

For the first time on my journey, I felt as if I was heading towards my end-point. Though I still had three more countries, and many hundreds of kilometres to travel, it felt as if I was now in the second half of my epic trip. I was really excited to be heading to the Balkans, a fabled land replete with mystery and intrigue that history had not always judged kindly.

And so to Serbia. What would I make of the country, its reputation so often sullied by events of the past? As I sat on the train, I felt a little uneasy. I didn't know how I would feel about entering a country that just twenty years or so before had been at the heart of a war, seen by many as the main perpetrators of ethnic cleansing so unspeakable that it beggared belief that this could have happened, effectively on our doorstep, a mere train journey away in Europe. Would the long-held animosities between various Balkan countries still be in evidence, the scars of the Great War a century before still affecting relations today between Serbia and Bosnia? How would the crimes of the Second World War, when Croatian *Ustaša* forces out-Nazi'd the Nazis, affect Croatia's relations with the Serbs now? And how would the unspeakable genocidal horrors of Sarajevo and Srebrenica following the break-up of Yugoslavia be felt among Croats, Bosnians and Serbs today? With their protracted history of myriad ethnic divisions and long-held grievances, I didn't quite know what the next three countries would have in store for me, but finding out was part of the reason for the trip.

I soon had more pressing concerns, however. The heatwave was showing no signs of relenting, and the greenhouse-like conditions of the train which I had put down to simply sitting in the station with its air-conditioning not yet fully operational were soon exposed as the de facto state of affairs. Within twenty minutes or so, it became quite clear that any air-conditioning this train may once have had was certainly not going to be in evidence for this trip, and with the afternoon sun starting to cascade in through the glass windows, the carriage was getting hotter and stuffier by the minute. Just as well I didn't have to attempt movements any more strenuous than opening a bottle of water for the next eight hours.

One of the joys of solo travel is that, with no co-traveller to converse with, no-one necessarily knows what nationality you are. Which means you can sit quietly and listen in to conversations that others have, should they happen to be in English. And so it was on the train to Belgrade. A few rows behind me, at a table of four, sat a group of Australians who – obviously better acclimatised to the heat than a pasty Scot like myself – felt able to chat away to each other whilst I tried not to do anything more strenuous than breathe for fear of passing out. They must have been of Greek origin as their conversation consisted of comparing the work ethic of Australians (like themselves) with that of family newcomers who had come to Australia in search of work following the most recent economic tribulations in Greece, and who seemed to have difficulty with adapting to a 9 a.m. start, a full day's work (every day) and no afternoon siesta! All very subjective of course, but it is part of the charm of travelling that you get to hear the views and musings of other cultures, and it provided some clandestine entertainment for me after not hearing English-speaking voices for such a long time.

The train rattled on at a languid pace through the Hungarian countryside and across the border into Serbia. It was becoming clear though, that we were not keeping to schedule, and the 8 p.m. arrival time was going to have come and gone with the train still meandering towards Belgrade. Not that I wasn't enjoying the journey – my reason for travelling by train was exactly that it is relaxed and enables the traveller to see more of the country than just the insides of departure lounges and airport concourses. And as darkness began to fall, so did the temperature, to a manageable level more akin to an oven than a blast furnace!

But with the fading of the day, so the next problem with the train was revealed – no lights. The guard came through and in very broken English (more hand-signals than verbal) explained that there was an electrical problem and hence the buffet car would be serving cold food only. Given that the train was running late, and I was starting to get hungry, I decided to make the effort to search for said buffet car, which I found, in pitch darkness but with all the windows wide open, facilitating a long-awaited and welcome blast of cool night air. I suspected, in terms of trade, that they had had better days.

My unsuspecting Australian companions decided to leave the train at the northern city of Novi Sad, but I chose to stay and get to Belgrade, having booked ahead for a hotel room which I hoped – with the train arriving so late – would still be waiting for me.

Arriving at Belgrade's central station, the place looked, if not deserted, then certainly as if someone was awaiting the arrival of our train so that they could then shut the doors and turn the lights off. Sometimes, though, you get a sense when you arrive somewhere new of a feeling of calm – you just know you're going to like this place – and so it was, this balmy night at a near-deserted railway station in the Balkans, I knew immediately that I was going to love Belgrade. Outside, a sparsely-populated taxi rank awaited, but the old Serbian driver who was there was the loveliest, friendliest taxi driver you could hope for, informing me – having ascertained my nationality – that I was the second Scotsman he had met that evening, his previous fare having apparently being a gentleman from Aberdeen. He pointed out to me that my hotel was in fact within relatively easy walking distance but I'd been on a train for ten hours with no electricity, no air conditioning and only meagre supplies and he seemed delighted to give me a run up the hill towards the centre of town where my hotel – hopefully – awaited, waving away with his hand my efforts to give him more than the token fare the short journey yielded. If all Serbs were as friendly and helpful as him, my preconceptions would be unfounded.

Thankfully, my hotel had kept my room for me, despite the late arrival. It was a small but modern hotel handily situated right on *Knez Mihailova*, the main pedestrianised thoroughfare in the centre of the old part of the city.

I dropped my bags, had a quick shower, and set about looking for something to fill my empty stomach. The reception staff quickly informed me that the hotel didn't offer dinner and that the kitchen, for any possible room service, was shut, it now being 11 o' clock at night. But not to worry, they assured me, there would be plenty of places still open at this time of night and I'd have no problem finding a place to eat. So, somewhat dubious, I set off out into the Belgrade night.

I'd read about Belgrade – which literally means 'the white city' – when I was planning the trip. 'Not pretty' was one of the recurring descriptors, with accounts of vast socialist-style buildings and housing blocks, though that was always caveated by tales of art nouveau masterpieces, remnants of the Habsburg legacy and past Ottoman influences. The other main descriptor was 'exuberant', with a reputation as a vibrant, chaotic party town brimming with life at all times of the day and night. It has been christened 'the Balkan New York' but that seemed a little ambitious to my mind and the comparison that seemed most appropriate to me was 'new Berlin', with its youthful and 'happening' vibe.

And, despite the late hour, that's exactly what I found as I stepped out onto the bustling *Knez Mihailova*, the street pulsating with people outside cafes, bars and restaurants, walking and laughing and enjoying the vibrancy of a warm summer's evening. It immediately felt safe too, the atmosphere one of enjoyment and vivacity where straightaway I felt at home and caught up in the mood.

The choice of eating and drinking establishments was plentiful, and after a while strolling and soaking up the atmosphere, I found a fabulous little fast-food eatery, obviously popular with locals, where the main offering seemed to be what's known as a *ćevapi*, a traditional Balkan snack of minced lamb or pork meat, onion, sour cream etc, wrapped in a flatbread with some salad. Not unlike a kebab, to be honest. And the popularity of this particular outlet seemed to be heightened by the fact that the 'meal deal' on offer was a kebab *and* a beer for what equated to about three euros. And so, nearing midnight on a bustling midweek night in central Belgrade, there I sat on my tall stool at a communal bench outside a busy *ćevabdžinica* grill shop, eating my delicious Balkan kebab and swigging a cold bottle of beer, watching the youthful crowds pass by me in all directions, and I knew I was going to enjoy my time in Belgrade.

A long walk east

Belgrade is a decent-sized city, some 1.2 million in population in the urban area and is located at the confluence of the Sava and the Danube (or *Dunav*) rivers. The historic centre of the city is at *Kalemegdan* on the right banks of both rivers, and the city expanded south and east over the centuries. On the left bank lies *Novi Beograd* (New Belgrade), a post Second World War construct which is now the central business district of the city. It is generally the older *Stari Grad* and *Centar Grada* parts of the city that will attract visitors more than the newer sprawls to the west, but Belgrade is characterised by an array of interesting little pockets to experience, such as Zemun quay, with its raft of bars, restaurants and nightlife, or *Ada Ciganlija*, an island on the Sava River in the heart of the city with an artificial lake, a long gravel beach and popular for bathing, barbeques, sports and picnics.

I'd turned westwards on my first night, walking up *Knez Mihailova* towards the Kalemegdan district by the rivers. The next morning though, I turned east and started on the long walk out towards probably the most iconic building in Belgrade, the beautiful *Svetog Save* Serbian Orthodox church.

My map suggested it would be about a 2.5 kilometre walk out to St Sava's, and with the heat still showing no signs of abating, I was happy to take it at a leisurely pace. The *Stari Grad* (Old Town) part of Belgrade around *Knez Mihailova* is a veritable mish-mash of architectural styles, some parts showing the remnants of the Ottoman influence, others conveying the elegance of the Habsburg period, and every so often I caught a glimpse of a blemish left over from the socialist period of the middle-to-late twentieth century. The pedestrian strip of *Knez Mihailova* itself features some beautiful and elegant buildings and mansions, and is a protected site, safeguarded as one of the oldest and most valuable landmarks in the city.

Soon the narrow chic lines of *Knez Mihailova* widened out to the busier and more functional *Terazije* area, where department stores sit side-by-side with hotels as the bustle of cars and taxis reminds you that you are in the heart of a capital city. Hotel Europa sits on what is romantically known as 'Pizza Corner', but a few hundred yards further down sits *Hotel Moskva*, one of the most beautiful and recognised buildings in Belgrade.

Built in a Russian style, this elegant hotel – the former Rossiya Palace – once towered over the city and was known as 'the giant house' and has been referred to as '*the most expensive and most beautiful Russian house in the Balkans*'. As with so many ornate buildings in Eastern Europe, this art nouveau icon of the city has had a turbulent history – variously commandeered as the Gestapo headquarters, nationalised by the communist leaders of Yugoslavia and now back operating as a privately-owned hotel. Its ceramic-tiled façade is especially impressive when lit up at night.

Continuing eastwards down *Terazije* brings you to the beautiful twin palaces of *Stari dvor* (the Old Palace) and *Novi dvor* (New Palace), set facing each other across immaculately manicured gardens. The Doric-columned *Stari dvor* was once a dynastic royal residence, and today houses the City Assembly; its architectural counterpart *Novi dvor* now houses the Office of the President of Serbia. The parterre style royal gardens, with a fountain between the two palaces, give the complex a formal and stately appearance and are a delightful spot to sit and admire the buildings. My one concern was the lack of shade – the Balkan heat in the middle of the day was unrelenting and I still had some distance to go to get to St Sava.

But at least I could now see it. The unmistakable white façade of the Orthodox church could be viewed in the distance as the *Terazije* road gave way to *Kralja Milana*, or 'The King's Street'. Standing in my way was *Trg Slavija*, a busy roundabout at the intersection of some of central Belgrade's major roads. I was interested to see it as, according to my guide book, a fellow Scotsman by the name of Francis Mackenzie built one of the first houses on this Slavija Square after the vast pond which had previously stood there had been drained and filled. Mackenzie was seemingly quite a prominent figure in Belgrade society at the end of the nineteenth century and was one of the major benefactors, in terms of land donation, to the construction of the St Sava church to the east. Crossing the roundabout was a feat in itself – eight roads intersect here, with cars, lorries, buses and trams all jostling for position, and traffic jams are commonplace. Apparently the city authorities have subsequently built a huge musical fountain in the centre of the roundabout, which has led to widespread ridicule. I wonder what the deeply religious Mr Mackenzie – who forbade both smoking and, bizarrely, the building of restaurants on his land – would have made of that.

The Temple of St Sava is the world's largest Orthodox church and the building dominates the skyline of Belgrade, the most famous building in the city. Originally commissioned in 1905, its construction stalled due to a succession of regional and world wars and the atheist rule of the Communists. It lay half-finished until permission was finally granted in 1985 for construction to recommence and the edifice was completed in 1989.

It is unquestionably a magnificent building, well worth the long walk. With its iridescent white marble and granite façade and multitude of green copper domes topped by golden crosses, it can reputedly host up to 10,000 worshippers at any one time, though the interior of the church is still not yet complete. The forty-nine bells in its towers announce noon each day. Framed against the flawless blue sky, you can see why this church is on a thousand picture postcards. It is a beautiful building and it is not hard to see why Serbs view it with such pride.

The church sits within Karadordev public park and the open spaces and greenery of the surroundings complement the grandeur of the church. The park also affords some valuable shelter from the incessant heat, with benches under the trees or in the shade of the National Library building providing a welcome reprieve from the baking sun.

One consequence of travelling solo is that you learn to be able to bluff your way through almost any situation. Sitting in the shifting shade observing the world go by, I watched as throngs of students entered and exited the library building which stands on the south side of the park and I decided to chance my arm. One thing I have always found is that, if you are trying to go somewhere where you sense you might not necessarily be allowed, it is best to attempt to do so with confidence and purpose. Dithering around, looking lost and trying to sneak into somewhere generally makes you stand out more. Purposefully striding into a building along with others tends to work so much better. And what's the worst that can happen? Someone approaches you and asks what you are looking for? Simple. Either be honest and say you're looking for the toilet/the café/whatever is appropriate, or fall back on the time-honoured tactic of playing the dumb tourist card. I once managed to gain entry, perhaps not necessarily shall we say by conventional methods, to an empty football stadium in South America that I – for reasons too elaborate to go into here – wanted to visit and take a photo of. Sitting in a stand, I was confronted by an armed security guard who seemed more surprised to see me almost than I was to see him, but a combination of showing him my camera and pointing to the rain outside led to him shrugging his shoulders and letting me remain. Nothing so dramatic behind my clandestine access this time though – I just wanted to use the toilets and get out of the burning sun for a while, and the library proved a convenient solution to both requirements.

In the same vicinity as St Sava, albeit not *that* close by, lay two other attractions that I was keen on. Firstly, the somewhat obscurely named House of Flowers is in fact the mausoleum to Marshal Josip Tito, former war partisan and President of Yugoslavia. Set within the grounds of the Museum of Yugoslav History, it is a curious 'must-see' on any trip to Belgrade, with displays and exhibits to a bygone era proving fascinating to anyone with an interest in life behind the Iron Curtain.

Secondly, near to the mausoleum and museum complex are the twin football stadiums of Belgrade – the *Stadion Partizan*, home to Partizan Belgrade, and the *Rajko Mitic Stadion* (formerly known as the *Marakana*), home to bitter rivals *Crvena Zvezda*, or Red Star Belgrade. For a football obsessive like myself, this was nirvana, getting to see the stadiums of clubs that, from my childhood, had such mythical names. The old Eastern European teams all had such grimly exotic names – Lokomotiv Leipzig, Dinamo Tblisi, Spartak Moscow, Carl Zeiss Jena. Names tended to come from where state affiliations lay – 'Lokomotiv' were the teams from the railway workers; 'Dinamo' tended to be linked to the state police; 'Spartak' from the trade unions; 'CSKA' or 'Steaua' belonging to the army. Similar divisions existed in Belgrade, with Partizan being aligned to the army and Red Star to the Interior Ministry. Matches between them, known as 'The Eternal Derby', were not what you would call friendly but to me, any chance to see famous football grounds is not to be passed up. I'd also read that the old *Marakana*, Red Star's ground, was the site (albeit in a previous iteration of the stadium) of the last-ever game played by the famous 'Busby Babes' of Manchester United before their ill-fated trip home via Munich.

Both stadiums are around a thirty to forty-five minute walk south from St Sava's, and after such a long walk out – 4 kilometres in the sweltering Balkan heat is not to be undertaken lightly – I'd strongly suggest taking the trolleybus (No.40 or 41) back into the city. And then finding somewhere quickly to consume an ice-cold beer.

A man in a fountain

Belgrade may not be the prettiest of cities in a purely aesthetic sense, but it does have its charms. I found the beauty to be more to do with the atmosphere, the vibe. It felt like a city that was alive and fun and, in my opinion, welcoming. That's not to say that it doesn't have pockets of loveliness – some of the parks and especially some of the churches are exquisite.

I certainly wasn't going to be venturing as far afield on my second day as I had on my first. The sights I chose to see were definitely much closer to the centre of the city after my

excursions out to the suburbs the day before. First on my list was
the impressive *Crkva Svetog Marka* (St Mark's Church), located
up past the parliament building, and reputed to be one of the
most striking buildings in Belgrade.

Built just before the Second World War, St Mark's is indeed
a beautiful building, its Byzantine-style construction of red-
tinted stone exterior creating a bold contrast to the many
grey, functional buildings that characterise much of Belgrade.
Inside, the church houses numerous priceless Serbian icons and
mosaics, but – as with St Sava's – apparently remains unfinished.
It seemed to me as if a bit of a theme was developing around
Serbian Orthodox churches in Belgrade. Just behind the majestic
Svetog Marka stands a tiny, but lovely, Russian Orthodox church
erected by refugees from the Russian Revolution, which is
equally worthy of a visit.

Adjacent to St Mark's you will find Tašmajdan Park, one of
downtown Belgrade's most popular locations. Bombed during
the NATO raids of the late 1990s, when sixteen people were
killed in the state television building which adjoined the park, it
has been rebuilt and re-established as a favourite haunt of locals
and visitors alike, with tree-lined paths and a stepped complex
of fountains popular with joggers and cyclists as well as those
seeking peace and tranquillity in the centre of a busy city. I was
more than happy to stroll through here and find a seat, in the
shade of the trees next to the fountains, to rest awhile and watch
the daily life of the city pass by.

Not everyone has the same idea about rest and relaxation I
guess. I say that because it was here that what I presume was a
local – and not an unfortunate homeless man as far as I could
tell either – decided on a rather unorthodox approach to cooling
down on this swelteringly hot afternoon. Fully clothed, he waded
into the fountain and plonked himself down directly under the
jets. Not satisfied with just getting a quick soaking to cool off,

he proceeded to sit there, quite happily, seemingly as contented in his seating arrangements as I was with mine. Before long, what I took to be a park guard came by and went over to him. Our aquatic friend swam to the side and conversed with the guard, in quite an animated style I may add, for a few minutes, then proceeded to paddle back to his preferred spot under the fountain with the guard seemingly powerless to do much to stop him. I had to admire his panache – it was certainly a novel way to cool down in the baking heat, though not a course of action I was going to replicate.

On the other side of St Mark's from the park, back towards the Old Town, stands the *Narodna skupština* (National Assembly building). Situated on Nikola Pašić Square, it is one of the most significant buildings in Belgrade. Built on the site of a huge Turkish mosque demolished immediately after Serbia gained independence from Turkish rule in 1878, it has served as the parliament building for Yugoslavia, then for Serbia and Montenegro and since 2006 for Serbia.

This area is very much the governmental and legislative quarter of Belgrade. Near to the National Assembly is the imposing but austere Palace of the Main Post Office, which is used as offices by some government ministries and also by the Constitutional Court of Serbia. Although designated a national monument, its harsh and unsmiling exterior put me more in mind of some of the secret police buildings I'd seen in Vilnius and Budapest. Directly across from the parliament is *Pionirski Park*, or Pioneers Park, through which leads you back to the old and new palaces of *Stari dvor* and *Novi dvor* that I had passed the day before.

For a city not given many plaudits in the guidebooks for its attractiveness, I have to say that this area – from the parliament through the parks to the old and new palaces – contains some mightily impressive buildings and which stand with the equals of any I'd seen on my journey so far. Don't let anyone tell you

Belgrade is not a pretty city. You just need to know where to look.

A taste of Montmartre, Balkan-style

One of the quirkiest areas to visit in Belgrade is that of *Skadarlija*. Similar to the Užupis district that I'd visited when in Vilnius, this historic neighbourhood of cobbled lanes and alleys is considered the bohemian quarter of the city and is often referred to as 'the Montmartre of Belgrade'.

Full of bars, cafes, restaurants, antique shops and art exhibitions, it has an ambience all of its own and is a wonderful place to spend time ambling and exploring the sights and sounds of this charming locality. I say 'locality' but it is in effect mainly just one long, winding, pedestrianised street with alleys and lanes off it, meandering its way downhill from the old centre of Belgrade. It is well worth the visit to get away from the hustle and bustle of the city and to feel almost like you are stepping back in time. As it has some great eating places, it is a popular option in the evenings too.

I also loved its street welcome sign, showing the layout of the area on a map with a little bit of a story beside it, giving the history of this idiosyncratic stretch of the city ('My name is Skadarlija…'). It is a nice touch for a city that seems very at ease with itself, a hidden treasure in more ways than one.

Cooling off in the Old Town

On the way back from *Skadarlija* to the Old Town, you pass through the student district of the city, with the buildings of the university surrounding a peaceful oasis in the middle known as *Studentski Trg*, or Students' Square. It was built on one of the oldest squares in Belgrade, and was envisioned to be the first of many squares on the central route from Kalemegdan to Slavija, though that plan never quite came to fruition. The square is now a park, filled with students at all times of the day and evening, either immersed in their books or deep in discussion, or just using the space to relax.

It's not the most beautiful of parks – more functional than pretty, with a grid-like layout and a good number of statues. But it is a peaceful oasis in a busy city, a pleasant and welcoming place to take a seat and watch the city go about its business. When you have been sightseeing and exploring a bustling city all day, it is always a welcome relief to find somewhere to sit in the shade, read a book and take the weight off your blistered feet for a while.

The last stop of the day though was back in the Old Town, to a contentiously named main square. Flanked on two sides by the National Theatre (built in a style reminiscent of La Scala in Milan) and the National Museum of Serbia, *Trg Republike* (Republic Square) is Belgrade's central square and main gathering point for locals and visitors alike. Populated by fountains and dominated by the statue of nineteenth century Serbian Prince Michael *(Knez Mihailo)* on his horse, the square is surrounded by cafes, bars and fast food outlets, adding to the sense that this is the beating heart of the city. The controversy over its name continues though, with many wanting the square renamed as either Freedom Square (after pro-democracy demonstrations were held here when Slobodan Milošević was in power in the 1990s) or simply back to one of its original names, that of Theatre Square. Whatever the name, it is a place where Belgraders tend to meet – either 'at the horse' or now more often 'at the clock' after the installation of a new public clock at the millennium.

My abiding memory of Republic Square, however, is that it is the only place I have ever been where the local authorities had laid on water trucks to enable people to cool down and rehydrate! With the searing temperatures showing no signs of abating, even the locals seemed to be withering in the heat and two large blue water trucks were parked on the square the afternoon I was there, with dispensers to fill up cups or water bottles or simply – as many seemed to be doing – splashing water on your hands and over your head and face to gain some respite from the sun.

I was happy with a more traditional way of cooling down – sitting in the shade of one of the many cafes and bars that surround the square and sipping a nice cold glass of beer. The Serbian *pivo* of choice goes by the name of *Jelen* and I'm not ashamed to say that the first couple of glasses went down barely touching the sides. Purely for rehydration purposes, you understand... Another initiative from the cafes of Belgrade that I welcomed was the cold water spray they attached to the oscillating air-conditioning fans, so that as I sat in the shade with my drink, I received an intermittent light misting of cool spray. For which I was hugely thankful.

When you sit with a drink, especially when you are on your own, you tend to notice other people, what the local characteristics are, how people behave in different cultures. Sitting with my beer on Republic Square, I couldn't help noticing two things. One, how chic and affluent a lot of the young Belgrade residents looked. And two, how just about everyone smoked – some regardless of whether they had a baby in a buggy at their side. It was something I'd noticed about Eastern Europe – the public smoking ban that you now find so much in the West had not caught on as yet in this part of the world and there seemed to be much less of a social stigma around smoking than has emerged in the last ten years or so in the UK, for instance. When I was in Poland a few years before, I could barely see the country for a haze of smoke – even the receptionist in my hotel was puffing away as he checked me in through a cloud of nicotine. Not that I was judging – each to their own, in my opinion. I've been to too many countries and seen too many differing cultural habits to start to criticise, and it's one of the joys of travel, to see how different cultures and different people live their lives.

All I cared about was that I was enthralled by Belgrade, and was so glad I'd found such an unheralded treasure of a city on my travels. I had one more day to go before I was on my way, continuing my journey south. But for this evening, I was happy to sit and relax and stroll the pedestrian streets of the Old Town and have another nice meal before my final day in this gritty and fun-loving city.

Fortress Belgrade

On my last day in Belgrade, I wanted nothing more than a 'down day', one which didn't involve rushing around but instead just gave me time to sit, relax and recharge my batteries. I was leaving the city that evening, so had had to check out of my hotel that morning, which was another reason not to be wandering too far or getting too hot and uncomfortable. So, having left my bags with the hotel porter and armed with my bare essentials for the day (a hat, a book and a bottle of water) I knew the ideal place to spend my last few hours in the city.

The citadel at Kalemegdan dates from Roman times, and the park and fortress which exist there today dominate this part of Belgrade. Located at the confluence of the Sava and the Danube rivers, this is Belgrade's 'Central Park' and is well worth the visit. It is a wonderful mixture of fortresses and ramparts, paths and walkways, shaded tree-lined hideaways inhabited by a playful population of squirrels, and filled with runners, walkers and elderly gentlemen immersed in their chess games.

Entering the complex from *Knez Mihailova* brings you into the park over the bridge and through the Karadjordje Gate. Kalemegdan as a whole is broadly split into the Upper Town *(Gornji Grad)* where the fortress and tree-lined pathways of the upper park are, and the Lower Town *(Donji Grad)* which slopes down via more open parkland to the rivers beyond.

The fortress itself is fascinating, with its rampart walls lined with tanks and cannons and the large military museum on one corner and the innocuous looking Ružica Church, with chandeliers made from spent First World War bullet casings, on another. It is also home to the Statue of the Victor, built to commemorate Serbia's victory over the Ottoman Empire (which might explain why the giant statue faces towards Austria!). The views over the rivers, to the districts of Novi Belgrade and Zemun beyond, and onwards towards the vast open plains of central Europe, are superb.

The lower park is also worth a visit. Much more open, it also comprises a zoo and a sports complex, plus Nebojša Tower, a former dungeon and cannon tower right by the river that now hosts a museum. The lower park is a great place to walk around, affording splendid views back up towards the fortress and also across the river.

My chosen spot, however, was a nice quiet seat in the tree-lined park where I could sit and read my book. Surrounded by chess players and squirrels, I was perfectly happy to have a few hours of doing nothing other than indulging myself, relaxing and enjoying the tranquillity and beauty of this delightful spot before I roused myself to head off and continue on the next leg of my journey south from the Baltic to the Balkans.

To leave as to arrive

My dilemma when planning this trip was how to get from Belgrade to Bosnia. Specifically, to the historic city of Sarajevo. I was trying to undertake as much of my journey as possible by train, but for this next leg, I seemed to be hitting the buffers.

Try as I might, I could not find any direct train between the two cities. There was an option to take a train from Belgrade to Zagreb and then on to Sarajevo, but that would involve two extended train journeys and a long wait for a connection, adding a frankly ridiculous thirty-one hours to my planned route. I'd also been told I could take a bus, but that that was not necessarily the most comfortable of options.

Just as I was about to bite the bullet on a lengthy or bumpy crossing, by chance I found a low-cost Serbian airline by the name of JetAir who operated a late night flight from Belgrade to Sarajevo. With a flight time of around an hour, and at a decent price too, this was a much more practical way of getting to my next destination. And if Michael Palin was allowed to 'cheat' and go by plane sometimes, then so could I. Especially when it was the only sensible alternative.

And so that evening, after my relaxing afternoon at Kalemegdan, I bade farewell to Belgrade and headed in a taxi towards the airport as the sun set on the city. My driver was an interesting guy, equally as friendly as the older gentleman who had welcomed me to Belgrade a few days earlier, who told me that he used to be a journalist for Reuters, based in Paris. He explained to me how difficult it had been, to be a Serbian abroad during the brutal Balkan Wars of the 1990s, especially in a journalistic community which reported on – and often experienced first-hand – the atrocities on the ground. He spoke with pride about the new nation that Serbia had become today, in his eyes a much younger, more vibrant, more outward-looking country than it had been twenty years before. He also took the opportunity to extol to me the virtues of Serbian women. 'Ukrainian women', he pronounced (on hearing that I'd come via Lviv) 'are beautiful, but only after one thing', rubbing his fingers together to suggest material gains. 'Serbian women', on the other hand, 'are every bit as beautiful but much more family-orientated, much more capable of making a man happy for life'. If he was trying to cajole me into finding a wife in Belgrade, he was leaving his pitch a bit late – we'd be at the airport in ten minutes.

Nikola Tesla Airport won't necessarily go down in the annals of my travel diaries as the most salubrious airport I've experienced. Nothing wrong with it per se, it was a perfectly modern and decent-sized airport. But just as I entered Serbia, so I left it, swapping a dark and un-air-conditioned train for an airport with defective plumbing. Let's just say the toilets were useable so long as you didn't need to flush or wash your hands, and we'll leave it at that.

But as I boarded the small plane, somewhat cross-legged, I did ruminate on my time in Belgrade and how much I had loved the city, the ambience and vitality and buzz of the place. And despite my reservations, I reflected on my delight in finding the people so friendly, welcoming and alive with the possibilities of the future rather than preoccupied with an inability to let go the disputes of the past. Would I find the same when I landed in the beautiful, unique but battle-scarred lands of Bosnia and Herzegovina? In a little more than an hour's time, I'd begin to find out.

*Temple of St
Sava, Belgrade*

*St Mark's Church
and Tašmajdan
Park, Belgrade*

*Water trucks
to cool down,
Belgrade*

The Old Palace (left) and the New Palace (right), Belgrade

A splash of colour,
Belgrade

The bohemian district of
Skadarlija, Belgrade

Kalemegdan Park and the Danube and Sava rivers from the Fortress, Belgrade

FIVE

BOSNIA

An island at the heart of Europe

didn't really know how to feel as I landed in Sarajevo.

On one hand, there was excitement. I was in another new country, one with such an eclectic character and evocative history, in a city that had captured my imagination when it hosted the Winter Olympics in 1984, hazy memories of British ice-skaters Torvill & Dean and American downhill skier Bill Johnson flitting through my mind. On the other hand, this had been the heart of a brutal and ethnically motivated war just a few years later, one I had watched with horror on the nightly news bulletins, a city besieged and brutalised before our very eyes. And I knew that the airport, and the roads nearby, had been the epicentre of the fighting and shelling from surrounding hills. Flying in to that airport, travelling these roads, made me feel a little uneasy, the images of the conflict still all too fresh.

It was dark, however, and late in the evening as I made my way eastwards along the long linear route from the airport to the historic centre of the city. I would go and visit the memorials, but for now I had to find my accommodation for the next few days, and start to get my bearings in a new city.

Being dropped off in the centre, the first thing that struck me was how similar the atmosphere was to the night I had arrived in Belgrade. Again, it was hot and humid – my God, it was sticky – and the streets were filled with locals sitting outside at the bustling bars and restaurants that lined the pedestrianised parts of central Sarajevo. My hotel was colourfully illuminated from the outside, the lights perhaps distracting from the slightly fading façade of what had been, undoubtedly, at one time a beautiful and grand old building. Though the hotel did seem to have been renovated internally to make it more of a health and fitness centre, there were still some rooms, down long dark corridors decorated by purple walls and deep-pile carpets. My room itself though was a treasure – I can't even begin to describe the shape, it had so many different angles, nooks and crannies, and I could not work out the ceiling configuration, with windows on high and in skylights which seemed more to resemble being lodged in a belfry. I loved it.

Well, apart from not being able to get any Wi-Fi reception on my phone, at least not without opening the door and holding my arm out into the corridor! But considering where I was, I couldn't help but remind myself that this was a mere first world problem. Overall, my initial impression of Sarajevo – of the people, the atmosphere of the city, of the quirky room and hotel – was one of warmth and I looked forward to exploring more of this remarkable city in the morning.

SARAJEVO

It is difficult to adequately describe Sarajevo. For one thing, by modern capital city standards, it is quite small with an urban population of less than 300,000. It had a very different feel to it compared with other cities I'd visited, a mix of vibrant old-style Ottoman, grandiose Austro-Hungarian and slightly morose Yugoslav socialism. It is also tightly wedged into a steep, narrow valley, surrounded by hills on three sides and elongated for miles along the modest Miljacka River. Dotted around the slopes of the surrounding hills are terracotta-coloured houses interspersed by countless minarets, which – come nightfall – are lit up to give a curious aura to the city, as if it is surrounded by a procession of candles or torchlights. Which may in fact, after the events here twenty years previously, be a fitting sensation.

Overall, though, the unmistakable impression I got of being in Sarajevo was that it did not feel like being in Europe. People say that it has a real 'East meets West' feel to it, but in my opinion with the minarets and mosques that surround the city and the Turkish influence of much of the historic centre, it feels as if you are much further south and east on the continent than you actually are. Which makes Sarajevo feel not just different, but special. Combined with the historic events and tragedy that have occurred here, it all adds up to being an intriguing and stimulating city to spend time in.

Remnants of a brutal war

There is no avoiding the fact that, though this city has many treasures, it is dominated by the events that occurred here between 1992 and 1996. For a period of 1,425 days, the city suffered the longest siege of a capital city in the history of modern warfare during the Bosnian War which followed the break-up of the old Yugoslavia.

I knew the unofficial name of the road that connected the historic centre of the city to the outer suburbs and the airport: 'Sniper Alley'. It is one of these terms that remain seared in the memory years after the event. Dominated in parts by high-rise buildings, this main boulevard saw civilians risk their lives on a daily basis during the conflict as snipers were able to pick off innocent victims just going about their normal business – over 200 were killed by sniper fire, many of them by a single shot to the head.

Many of the buildings – shelled, bullet-ridden or destroyed by fire – have been renovated or rebuilt, including the famously-yellow former Holiday Inn hotel which became the front-line home of the international media covering the siege.

Beyond the airport, in the basement of a non-descript house in the district of Butmir, is possibly the most fascinating remnant of the war – the entrance to the Sarajevo Tunnel, an 800 metre stretch of covered trenches and underground tunnels hand-dug under the airport runway in 1993 to connect the besieged city, surrounded by hostile Serbian forces, to the outside world. This tunnel provided a lifeline to move food, arms and people and kept Sarajevo supplied during nearly four years of siege. The museum offers a fascinating and deeply moving insight into the construction of the tunnel, how it was guarded and how its location was kept secret and safe from Serbian shelling, and enables visitors to walk through a 25 metre long restored section of the tunnel, just 1 metre wide and 1.6 metres in height. You can get here by public transport (though it is convoluted in the extreme), by taxi or on an organised tour, but however you make it, I would urge anyone to do so and to marvel at the ingenuity and fortitude shown by those involved.

Near to Sniper Alley is the Vrbanja Bridge, another deeply poignant reminder of the futility of war. It was here that two young childhood sweethearts – Boško Brkić, a Serb, and his Bosnian Muslim girlfriend Admira Ismić – were shot as they attempted to cross the bridge and escape the besieged city. At around 5pm on 19 May 1993, a bullet hit Boško and killed him instantly. Another shot was fired and Admira fell to the ground, wounded but not killed. Instead of trying to flee, she crawled over to her boyfriend, lay down beside him, hugged him, and died. According to reports from observers at the time, Admira remained alive for at least fifteen minutes after the shooting.

The bodies of Admira and Boško lay on the bridge for eight days, as both sides argued over who had killed them, with no-one daring to enter the 'no man's land' to recover them. Christened by the world's media as 'the Romeo and Juliet of Sarajevo', the two are now buried, side by side, in Lion Cemetery, surrounded by thousands of other victims from the siege of Sarajevo. To this day, it is not known with certainty who fired the shots that killed them.

It is the one thing that strikes you most about Sarajevo – the preponderance of graveyards that dominate the hillsides surrounding the city. I've visited the huge cemeteries of Normandy for the D-Day landings; I've toured Flanders and the Somme on the Western Front and been overwhelmed by the countless cemeteries that dot the fields and farmlands of the region. But I wasn't prepared for Sarajevo, looking up over the hillsides and seeing a sea of spotless white headstones everywhere I looked.

More than 10,000 died here during the Balkan War, including an estimated 1500 children. The siege of the city didn't end until February 1996, despite the war officially ending with the signing of the Dayton Accord in December 1995. In a small park on *Maršala Tita* street stand two remembrance memorials – a glass monument and a beautiful fountain to commemorate the children slain during the fighting, and adjacent, seven grey metallic cylindrical columns inscribed with the individual names of 521 children who were killed during the siege. Having walked amongst the war graves of both the First and Second World Wars, I had seen rows and rows of memorials for soldiers aged seventeen, eighteen and nineteen. But reading the names and dates on the Memorial for the Children of Sarajevo, seeing so many, so young, with dates of 1992, 1993, 1994, 1995… It was so chillingly close in history. I could almost sense it as I stood there wondering how on earth this could have happened in the heart of the European continent.

Watching the people of Sarajevo go about their daily business, the city bustling away behind me, I wondered how they could have put something so traumatic behind them and how they contained the resentment, anger and desolation that must affect them. On the surface, this is just any other modern city. But all around are the unnerving reminders of a brutal, and all-too-recent, past.

Standing in the footsteps of history

There is a danger, if you are not careful, of concentrating solely on this recent history but that would cloud the many other charms this magnetic city holds: the architecture, the diversity, the vibrancy, and indeed, the somewhat old-world charm, the sensation of being far from where you know you actually are.

All along the river, an eclectic mix of architectural styles pervades the buildings. The stunningly ornate Central Post Office; the Academy of Fine Arts (a former Evangelical Church and one of the most beautiful buildings in Sarajevo); the white-colonnaded National Theatre; the Moorish façade of the National Library (and former City Hall); the ornate Ashkenazi Synagogue; and the classically Ottoman-styled Emperor's Mosque, the largest single sub-dome mosque in Bosnia and Herzegovina, all stand on the river's side and all of them are well worth visiting. As is the *Festina Lente* pedestrian bridge, with its quirky loop-in-the-middle modernist style. I took shelter from the sun and grabbed a seat, drink and bite to eat in the *At Mejdan* park, and looked over to the spot that had traditionally been the reason why the name of Sarajevo was so well-known.

As every school textbook recounts, the assassination of Austrian Archduke Franz Ferdinand in June 1914 was the catalyst for the start of the Great War, triggering as it did the progression from a complex set of alliances and ententes to the inevitability of hostilities. And just across *Latinska ćuprija* (Latin Bridge) was the exact spot where the assassination took place. As history tells us, a group of amateur assassins linked to the Serbian nationalist 'Black Hand' society awaited the royal motorcade and tried – and initially failed – to blow up the convoy with a grenade. Fate, however, presented a second chance with the motorcade taking a wrong turn and getting boxed in by the river, allowing a nineteen year-old by the name of Gavrilo Princip the opportunity to aim his pistol and shoot both Ferdinand and his wife Sophia dead, thus setting off a chain of events that led to the outbreak of the First World War a matter of weeks later.

A museum (Sarajevo Museum 1878-1918) now stands of the corner by the assassination site, a small but hugely interesting exhibition documenting the era of Austro-Hungarian rule in Bosnia and Herzegovina up to and including the Great War, and including photos and replicas from the Archduke Ferdinand assassination. For any history buff, it is well worth a visit.

A trip to the Olympic complex

The next morning, I wanted to go and visit some of the sights that had lodged Sarajevo in my head as a sports-mad teenager. The 1984 Winter Olympics were held in Sarajevo, then part of Yugoslavia, and as a fourteen year-old I had watched avidly the coverage afforded by what was at that time a solely terrestrial British TV network consisting of a meagre four channels. Sarajevo seemed so far away, so grimly exotic to me at the time, not somewhere I would ever have thought I would travel to. All I had known of the city before that was the vague memory of one of the best Yugoslavian international football players at the 1982 World Cup being called Safet Sušić and knowing he had played for FK Sarajevo before being one of the few Eastern European players allowed to transfer to a Western club when he signed for Paris Saint-Germain.

My sporting pilgrimage was to be two-fold. I wanted to visit the Olympic arena, but that was further out of town so could wait until later. First though, was to track down and visit the indoor arena where the ice hockey, speed-skating and crucially the ice dancing had taken place. Britain's Jayne Torvill and Christopher Dean were, in these days, the sporting superstars of the nation and by 1984 were completing their hat-trick of World Championship titles and seeking an Olympic Gold with their famous 'Bolero' routine.

The purported site of their Gold medal performance was, according to my map, at the Olympic Complex Skenderija, on the banks of the Miljacka River a little way west from the centre. Originally built as a cultural and sports centre in the late 1960s, it was expanded into a supposed state-of-the-art ice sports venue for the 1984 Olympics, to complement the new venues built further up the hill at the main Olympic complex. Thirty years later, however, on the swelteringly hot morning that I tracked it down, I was more disturbed by the sign on the doors of the shopping centre that sits beneath the arena – the large red warning signage alerted me to the fact that I could not enter the shopping mall with a dog, a bike or... a gun. Good to know.

Upstairs, the Olympic hall looked as if it might have seen better days, and was in a severe state of refurbishment. Never one to allow a few workmen or scaffolded trade entrances put me off a mission, I innocently sauntered in to the empty venue and found my way up the deserted stairs until a door took me into the arena. There, sitting in a row of wooden bucket-seats,

I looked out over the arena below and imagined the strains of Maurice Ravel's music echoing out as Britain's finest ice skaters finished their performance to rapturous applause and a sea of perfect 6.0 scores.

Except that I was actually in the wrong place. Apparently this venue had only hosted the ice hockey. The venue where Torvill and Dean had won their Gold medal was actually the purpose-built Zetra arena next to the Olympic stadium. How pleased I was to discover that fact on my return home...

Still blissfully ignorant of my mistake, I left the tired old arena and set about finding the main Olympic stadium which my map showed me was a mile or so out of town in the hills to the north of the city. The heat was showing no signs of relenting though, and after some time walking I found myself at the foot of the long and uphill *Alipašina ulica*, the thought of walking out of town, up a hill in the heat to a venue I wasn't entirely sure I knew how to find, led me to the realisation that this was why taxis had been invented. My driver wasn't the most communicative of chaps, and the combination of my rudimentary language skills and pointing to the Olympic complex on the map merely seemed to elicit a look of confusion from him, and when he repeated 'Olimpijski stadion?' to me a couple of times I couldn't help but notice the questioning tone in his voice. Maybe he just wasn't used to people asking him to take them there. Maybe he just thought I was lazy. Unperturbed, off we set, up the hill and out of the centre of town and into the hillside suburbs.

On being dropped off – my taxi u-turning with indecent haste and haring away back down the hill into town – I could see why my driver had been so quizzical. The Olympic complex was pretty desolate. Even on a blisteringly hot and sunny summer's day, the place looked bleak and deserted. I had hoped, in the manner of my South American stadium break-in experience, that there may have been a sneaky way into the Asim Ferhatović Hase Olympic stadium, but no. Despite walking all the way around the typically Communist-era concrete bowl, I could find no obvious entrance and therefore had to console myself with a snatched photo through a gap into the empty green-seated stadium that had once hosted an Olympic games.

Next to the stadium stand other remnants from the Olympics, including a tower still adorned with the multi-coloured and interconnected Olympic rings, and the Zetra Arena (now renamed after the former International Olympic Committee president Juan Antonio Samaranch), where my journey to retrace the steps of Torvill and Dean *should* have taken me. Even here though, there is scant escape from the vestiges of war. The Zetra Arena had been used as a morgue during the siege of the city, the wooden seats used to make coffins for the thousands killed. Even some of the surrounding land had been turned over for use as cemeteries – the St Mark's cemetery, St Joseph's cemetery and the aforementioned Lion cemetery being joined by the Stadium cemetery in the shadow of the arena. In fact, from here, high up on the plateau above Sarajevo, the plethora of cemeteries was all too palpable, hundreds and thousands of white headstones unmistakably evident in all directions.

When I came home, I found a few articles online about the broken legacy of the 1984 Olympics, showing photos of so many of the (mainly mountain) venues which now lie empty and abandoned, overgrown and derelict, a million miles away from the headlines of the bobsleigh and downhill skiing that captured the world's attention back in 1984. At least the Zetra – or Samaranch – Arena is back in operation, and the Olympic stadium itself – even though I couldn't manage any form of access – has been reconfigured into a sleek 37,000 capacity stadium, home to two city football teams and to the international matches of the Bosnian national football team. Regardless, I will always have fond and emotive memories of these Games and I am grateful that I had the opportunity to visit.

In the soul of the city

For my last day in Sarajevo, I wanted to wind down and take things at a more relaxed pace. A morning hike up to the Yellow Bastion had left me shattered. Part of the old city walls, it offers unrivalled views back down the valley over the city and it is not hard to see why it is one of the most popular vantage points in Sarajevo. The walk back is manageable, even in the baking heat of a Balkan summer, but the journey up may have been better by taxi or one of the minibuses that seemed to shuttle up and down from the city below.

I needed the afternoon to be more sedate and the ideal locale to do just that is by lazily ambling through the beguiling Old Town district, soaking up its old-world feel. It is here that you recognise just how cosmopolitan Sarajevo really is, a diverse melting pot of different cultural influences from Sarajevo's past, a kaleidoscope of Ottoman and Austro-Hungarian buildings and peoples all coinciding with each other. The fact that I visited Sarajevo during the Islamic Festival of Eid, which marks the end of Ramadan, just added to the atmosphere.

The narrow streets felt more like walking through a market or bazaar, with stalls and cafes and courtyards in abundance. Mosques mingle with churches and synagogues to highlight why Sarajevo has often been referred to as 'the Jerusalem of the Balkans'. The best way to explore this area is just to put your map back in your pocket and wander aimlessly through the narrow streets and alleyways, following the sights and smells of this fabulous district.

Ferhadija is the main thoroughfare which runs through the Old Town district, and it is from here that you can marvel at buildings such as the grandly named Cathedral Church of the Nativity of the Theotokos, the largest Serbian Orthodox church in Sarajevo and one of the largest in the Balkans. Close by is the *Katedrala Srca Isusova*, the Cathedral of the Sacred Heart of Jesus. More commonly referred to just as Sarajevo Cathedral, it is the largest Christian church in the Balkans. On the concourse in front of the church stands a statue of Pope John Paul II who visited the city in 1997 to preach for peace and tolerance following the war. Adding to the theistic complement is the Old Jewish Temple (or Old Synagogue) which has survived since the end of the sixteenth century despite fires, looting and Nazi occupation and is now a designated national monument. It is here that Sarajevo's Jews were detained before being deported to concentration camps.

The most important architectural reminder of Ottoman rule in the city is however the *Gazi Husrev Beg* mosque, the main congregational place of worship for Muslims in Bosnia and Herzegovina. More than just a mosque, it is an entire complex also comprising a religious school, a bazaar and a small observatory, as the elegant stone Old Clock Tower is apparently the only public clock in the world that keeps lunar time to indicate the calling of daily prayers. According to this system, each new day begins at sunset, when the time is shown as 12:00, hence the clock always looks as if it is telling the wrong time.

Continuing along *Ferhadija* leads you out onto the jewel in the crown of Sarajevo's Old Town, the bustling square at *Baščaršija*, often referred to as 'Turkish Town' because of its byzantium atmosphere. Probably the most touristy place in the city, this old market place dates from the fifteenth century and was the trading centre of the old city. Today, it is a captivating place to spend some time, with traditional food stalls and street cafes in abundance, though beware – the nickname of 'Pigeon Square' is not unwarranted!

In the middle of the square is *Sebilj*, an ornate mix of a monument and fountain which derives its name from an Arabic custom of providing water for the poor and needy. All around, and in the narrow alleyways leading off, you can find a variety of gastronomical delights in the numerous cafes and *buregdžinicas*, Sarajevo's answer to fast-food outlets selling traditional pita dishes such as *burek* (meat filled); *zeljanica* (spinach); *krompiruša* (potato); *sirnica* (cheese); and *tikvenica* (squash). My nose, however, led me to try some *ćevapi* – rolled spiced meat balls served with pitta-bread, onions and yoghurt and considered to be the national meal of Bosnia – which were delicious.

Sitting here with my lunch, I watched the vibrant and cosmopolitan flow of people and felt a million miles away, in Istanbul or North Africa maybe, but certainly a world away from what had been an ethnic warzone just a few years earlier. I was loving Sarajevo, its distinctive ambience and inimitable charm, its history and legacy of triumph over adversity, and I was saddened that my time here was coming to a close.

Panoramic view from Yellow Bastion over Sarajevo

Old City Hall and National Library, Sarajevo

*Legacies of war: War memorial with the names of some of the
1500 children killed during the siege of Sarajevo between 1992 and 1996 (left)
and the hillsides covered with graves (right)*

*The quirky Festina Lente Bridge (left) and the historic Latin Bridge
(next to where Archduke Franz Ferdinand was assassinated in 1918)
over the Miljacka River, Sarajevo (right)*

Baščaršija market place, Sarajevo

It was an early departure from Sarajevo. The journey to the station at dawn, with the roads being swept and the sight of the city being prepared for a new day, left me – once again – with a feeling of melancholy at leaving another remarkable stop on my journey.

The train to Mostar was a local train, and not especially busy. A few backpackers were clearly taking the same route as me, two Australian girls chatting away to each other a few seats in front of me. The solitude suited me though – I'm never great company at that time of the morning even at the best of times – and the scenery was company enough.

The journey – around two and a half hours – initially meandered through the greener, more forested valleys closer to Sarajevo but the terrain soon gave way to a much more arid, barren mountain landscape as the train headed south through Herzegovina. The sparsely populated topography of rough-hewn mountains and beautiful river valleys, reminded me in some ways of the Scottish Highlands, and that helped make me feel more at home after weeks away. Soon enough we had picked up the course of the Neretva River and followed its path as the mountains gave way to a wider valley and the outskirts of Mostar came into view. My next stop was within reach.

MOSTAR

Arriving at the small station, a few hardy souls stepped off the train and headed down the hill and over the bridge towards the centre of town. It was only 9.30 a.m. but I could already tell that it was going to be a monumentally hot day.

I'd booked a small B&B, a little villa of six or seven rooms that had been recommended to me. I knew the address and reckoned that as Mostar was not that big, and I had a map, I could find it easily enough by foot. However the half-hour or so it actually took me to locate the villa left me pretty dehydrated, and I was thankful to drop off my bags and get into the welcome cool of the air conditioning for a while. Unpacked and refreshed, I wandered back downstairs, ready to head off for the day, only to be met by my host who looked at me aghast. 'You're not going out in this heat?' she exclaimed, looking at me as if I was certifiable. Well yes, I replied, I was only here for a couple of days and I wanted to go out and see the city. 'Oofft, I stay here with the air conditioning' she retorted, her expression and dismissive wave of the hand saying it all with regard to her views as to my imminent excursion. I'd be fine. I had a hat. It couldn't be that hot...

Straight to the bridge

Mostar literally translates as 'bridge-keeper' and the town grew up around the crossing of the strategically-important Neretva River. The most iconic sight, the one reason why Mostar has for centuries attracted so many visitors, is the magnificent *Stari Most* (Old Bridge). Built in 1566, this magnificent stone arch bridge quickly became the symbol of the city, a wonder of medieval engineering in the powerful and fast-growing Ottoman Empire. The traveller Evliya Çelebi wrote in the seventeenth century: '*the bridge is like a rainbow arch soaring up to the skies, extending from one cliff to the other. ...I, a poor and miserable slave of Allah, have passed through 16 countries, but I have never seen such a high bridge. It is thrown from rock to rock as high as the sky.*'

And there it stood, in all its majesty, defying regional wars and even occupation by Italian Axis forces during the Second World War, for 427 years until November 1993, when – in one of the most depressingly pointless acts of the Yugoslav civil wars – it was purposely shelled and destroyed by Croatian artillery fire.

I remember watching the TV pictures of the destruction on the evening news, seeing the bridge – already brutalised and near-decimated by tank fire – being hit on one of its standing pillars and the whole edifice crumbling within seconds and collapsing into the river below. It seemed such a symbolic act, the intentional destruction of possibly the most recognisable image of Bosnia and Herzegovina, by fighters who until a year earlier had been allies, friends, neighbours. The pointlessness of the act, the realisation that it was gone, 400 years of history destroyed in an instant. It was heart-breaking.

Following the end of the war in 1995, huge progress was made in the reconstruction of the city of Mostar and in 1999, a major project was initiated to rebuild the bridge in its original design and to restore surrounding structures and neighbourhoods. A five year long programme of in-depth rehabilitation concluded in July 2004 with the grand opening of the rebuilt bridge in its fully restored former glory, and a year later both the bridge and surrounding areas were designated as World Heritage Sites by UNESCO.

And it is a quite magnificent bridge. Spanning a narrow gorge in the Neretva River, it connects the two halves of the Old Town and is once again the centrepiece in promoting Mostar as a cultural and tourist destination, able to be viewed and photographed from a dozen different angles on both sides of the bank. It is also home to the Bridge Divers' Club, where members (after collecting enough donations from the throngs of tourists who gather to watch) dive off the bridge and elegantly plunge into the waters below. Visitors can also attempt the dive, after some rudimentary training and hiring of equipment, but it was fair to say that I was happier on the sidelines watching.

Getting the best view of the bridge, and of the divers, can be tricky as the bridge itself – certainly when I was there – is mobbed with tourists. I decided to make my way down to the stony river bank below, where I hoped there would also be some shelter and shade. I have to admit, in all my years on this earth I have never, ever known heat like that day by the bridge in Mostar. The electronic clock I saw later showed the temperature as 44°C (a mind-blowing 111°F). I was all but melting; I had water seeping out of pores on parts of my body that I didn't even know *could* sweat. Even with a hat and enough sun-block to paint the Forth Bridge, it was almost impossible to stay out in the direct sun for more than a few minutes. Down by the river at least were some trees, but finding a space beneath them was complicated by the fact that everyone was having the same idea and sometimes the best you could hope for was the shade of a few outer leaves until someone moved on and you could grab their sheltered spot. Nonetheless, the sight of the bridge, restored to its original glory and attracting so many people back to the town, was reward enough and made the discomfort of the heatwave eminently worthwhile.

Along the cobbled alleys

Although *Stari Most* grabs all the attention in Mostar, a short walk away on the western bank brings you to another – equally as ancient and almost as beautiful – bridge, that of *Kriva ćuprija*, also known as 'the Sloping Bridge' or 'Crooked Bridge'. Crossing a narrow creek off the main river, this stone single-arch bridge was rumoured to have been built a few years *before* the Old Bridge, as a sort of test project before the main bridge was constructed. It was also destroyed and rebuilt in the early part of this century, though by floods rather than war. Today, it is still surrounded by old stone mill houses, many of which are now converted into cafes and small restaurants.

On the other side of the Old Bridge lies the beautifully restored old Ottoman quarter, its cobbled lanes and alleys filled with trinket sellers and tourists. Once the site of an old bazaar, the main attraction is undoubtedly *Kujundžiluk* (Gold Alley), a narrow cobbled lane with vendors on either side selling any number of treasures, a veritable maze of souvenir stalls, craft shops and cafes. Numerous restaurants can be found around here too, and the place is as busy at night as it is during the day. The major selling point for these eateries is that from their *tabhana*, the enclosed courtyards that used to house the tanneries that dotted the river bank, you can sit and enjoy superb views of the Old Bridge whilst you eat. I found I never tired of those views.

As with Sarajevo, the skyline in Mostar is dotted with minarets from the numerous mosques that inhabit the town, and two of the most accessible are located in the Old Town. Right on the river is the Koski Mehmed-Pasha Mosque which allows access both to the mosque itself and to the beautiful courtyard where you can enter and respectfully take photos free of charge. And – if you have a head for heights and don't suffer too badly from claustrophobia – you can also climb the minaret for superb views over the river and the Old Town. And just a short stroll further on brings you to the Karadjoz-bey Mosque, the biggest and arguably most beautiful mosque in the region, with its huge dome and tall minaret. In keeping with much of Mostar, the mosque was almost completely destroyed during the civil war and has since been lovingly rebuilt and reopened.

I took a slight detour up some narrow side street alleys to locate *Sahat kula*, the 15 metre high square stone Clock Tower which has stood since the mid-1600s. Impressive as it is, I was disappointed in not being able to climb up it, though with the heat of the day still as intense, that was probably a blessing in disguise.

Back down in the main thoroughfare, the end of Gold Alley leads into *Braće Fejića*, Mostar's main shopping street and home to many of the city's hotels and guest houses. Further on, you arrive at *Trg Musala*, once the heart of Austro-Hungarian Mostar but now home to a fountain surrounded by gardens and, to be honest, not much else.

Mostar is beautiful, but most of the beauty is concentrated around the small area of the Old Bridge and Ottoman Quarter. However, some of the street food you can buy is divine – I treated myself to *burek* from one stall, a slice of pastry filled with spicy meat and onions, a bit like what in England you might consider similar to a pasty or in Scotland a bridie, though this Bosnian *burek* came more like a slice of pie. Either way, it was amazing. And the stallholder seemed amused at me, having wolfed down the first one and coming back to ask for a second. Well, I was just appreciating an authentic regional delicacy!

A contentious reminder

Mostar is a complex place. On one level, you have the tourists back in force and the bridge being photographed from every angle, and the whole setting – in a picturesque river valley with barren hills rising above – is so peaceful and idyllic. But again, the reminders of a brutal and turbulent near past are never very far away.

Despite so many of the buildings and attractions having been rebuilt, with painstaking care to recreate the original look, you don't have to look too far to see reminders of the destruction that all but decimated the city in the early 1990s. I read that of the twenty-seven Ottoman-era mosques in the city of Mostar, twenty-six of them were destroyed or badly damaged during the fighting. Bullet marks and shell fire holes are still evident on some of the buildings away from the old Ottoman quarter, with the area around *Spanski Trg* (Spanish Square), not actually very far from the end of the tourist area, still showing signs of the decimation that occurred, the skeleton remains of the old Ljubljanska Banka building the most visible.

The most contentious reminder of all though looms large over the city. A 100-foot tall cross stands atop Hum Hill, which overlooks Mostar. The cross, of course, is a Christian symbol, not an Islamic one, and it illustrates the divide in the city that still to some degree exists. Although the mainly Muslim Bosniaks and Catholic Croats were initially united in fighting for their respective independence against the Serb-dominated Yugoslavia, it wasn't long before the former allies turned against each other in a complex internecine conflict. It was the Croats that shelled and destroyed the iconic *Stari Most* bridge, and it was from Hum Hill that much of the shelling of the city originated as the Croats and Bosnians fought each other and the city became partitioned along ethnic lines. Erecting the giant cross on Hum Hill is seen as offensive and deeply insensitive to the Muslim Bosnian residents, an unnecessary reminder of the deaths of nearly 2,000 people. The Croatians, for their part, view the cross as a commemorative symbol for those lost during the war.

However the rights and wrongs are viewed, what seems incontestable is that the visible nature of the monument acts as a stark reminder that, despite the peace and accommodation that came about following the end of the war, the old tensions do not lie far beneath the surface. And for such a beautiful and historic place, that seems the enduring tragedy.

The iconic Old Bridge, Mostar

Bridge-diving, Mostar

Reminders of the war, Mostar

Views from the Old Bridge across the Neretva River
to the Ottoman Quarter and Old Town, Mostar

SIX

CROATIA

Destination Dubrovnik

L eaving Mostar was hard. It was not just that I was leaving such a beautiful place, but also that I was leaving Bosnia and Herzegovina, which I had loved from the moment I had landed in Sarajevo. Such an amazing country, with such beautiful wild countryside and friendly people, with its unique history and culture, it truly felt like an island in the midst of my journey.

And I was sad too that this was to be the last leg of my epic voyage. Croatia would be my last stop before heading home, and a journey that had felt at times as if it had taken me a million miles away was now coming to a close. My journey from the Baltic Sea to the Balkan Coast was nearing its conclusion, but my instinct was to look back, to the way I'd come, rather than to look ahead to the journey's end.

My options for getting to Dubrovnik were again limited, as no direct trains ran from Mostar to the Adriatic Coast. Taking a bus was the most viable option and, on checking the timetables, it seemed to be a three or four hour journey. However, my host at the little villa where I was staying had another option for me – I could get a lift down with one of her colleagues by car the next day which would cut the journey to a little over two hours. And so, after a final hearty Bosnian breakfast, off we set.

The countryside south of Mostar was again quite barren, but still staggeringly beautiful, and as the road swept down past hills and through valleys on our way to the coast, I reflected on the little farmhouses and small villages we drove through, looking at the people we passed and imagining the life they had seen. All of this area had experienced fighting during the civil war, often worse, with villages cleansed and ethnic divisions exploited. How many of these faces had seen friends and family killed, how many near neighbours had become enemies as they turned and fled to congregate in new territories along religious, ethnic and nationalistic lines?

The road skirted around the border of Republika Srpska, the largely autonomous Serb-controlled region which forms one of the two legal entities – along with the Federation of Bosnia and Herzegovina – that makes up the delicately balanced and somewhat artificially-constructed country we tend to simply call 'Bosnia'. I wanted to ask my driver how relations were between the two parts of the country, how people in this region viewed this bizarre construct, if peace and relative normality had been restored. I knew the Republika Srpska had spawned two notorious figures – ex-President Radovan Karadžić, sentenced to forty years' imprisonment in 2016 on charges of war crimes, genocide and crimes against humanity by an International Criminal Tribunal at The Hague, and the notorious former Bosnian-Serb General Ratko Mladić, jailed for life for genocide and other atrocities in 2017 (bizarrely, as I was writing this chapter).

I always found it hard asking my hosts questions such as these – I could tell how raw the emotions still were. My driver, Adnan, told me that there was still much suspicion between the two areas, that the Serbs kept themselves very much to themselves and that there were often problems for non-Serbs returning to live in towns and villages now annexed to a different administrative entity, and that he feared, in time, the Serbs would push for Republika Srpska to become part of a wider 'Greater Serbia'. When I asked if he had been impacted by the fighting during the civil war, he merely replied 'Yes'. I felt it best not to push him further. Perhaps the fact that my Bosnian was limited to simple key phrases and his English was good but not comprehensive, was a blessing. Once again though it made me reflect on what horrors and upheavals this small country had had to endure – so recently, and in such close proximity to the peace and freedoms we take for granted in the surrounding countries of Western Europe.

Before long, the shimmering waters of the Adriatic could be glimpsed in the distance as we approached the Croatian border. It was the first time I had seen the sea for weeks, having been land-locked in Central and Eastern Europe since I left the Baltic in Lithuania. It struck me again that this was the end-point to my epic journey from one end of Europe to the other, and that made me melancholy. I'd seen so many amazing places, interacted with so many wonderful people, and seen so many towns, cities and countries that had been hidden from view for so many decades but which all had so much history, so much vitality, so much beauty to be explored. As we entered the bustling tourist port of Dubrovnik, the remoteness of Lviv and the overnight train journeys through the wide plains of western Ukraine now seemed like a different world and a long, long way away.

DUBROVNIK

The first thing you notice about Dubrovnik is how busy it is. In all the towns and cities I'd visited on my trip south, maybe only Budapest could be described as 'touristy', and even then only in certain areas. But Dubrovnik screamed of tourists from the first moment we entered the town – cruise ships lining the harbour, signs for hotels in all directions, people walking about in shorts and flip-flops. Not that this is necessarily a bad thing, but after so many quiet or traditional settings populated mainly by locals, the bustle and transient feel did come as a bit of a culture shock.

The main change was the language. For the first time in weeks, I was hearing the English language spoken frequently, with Australians, Americans, Irish and Brits strolling through the town and conversing in my native language. It is an interesting aspect of travelling alone, one that I also experienced on long trips through South America and South-East Asia, that you get used to not hearing your own language spoken and not having any meaningful conversation with another person for weeks on end. And as a consequence, the only conversations you tend to have are in your own head – a form of inner monologue, a series of running commentaries and observations with yourself as you experience new places and people or sit alone at dinner in a faraway land. It can initially be quite disconcerting, though you soon get used to it and I've found that I've often grown to enjoy the peace and privacy it affords. And when you are parachuted back into a world where noise and other people's conversations and plans are expressed vocally for you to hear, it can feel a bit intrusive, as if someone has just invaded your own little private world.

And so it was in Dubrovnik. The days of being a traveller alone had ceased, and I was now back deep in tourist territory! Dropped off at my charming little bed and breakfast, I bade farewell to Adnan as he headed off on his business before returning across the border and home to Mostar. For me, it was time to sample the delights of one of the jewels of the Adriatic coast and a city replete with its own attractions and diverse history before I myself headed home.

My guide book told me that Dubrovnik had a population of just 42,000, though clearly that number swells greatly during the summer tourist season. Historically a key maritime trade port, the Old Town and city walls became a UNESCO World Heritage site in 1979, when still part of the old Yugoslavia. In fact, throughout the 1980s Dubrovnik was a hugely popular destination for British holiday-makers and doesn't therefore fall into the category of 'undiscovered treasure' that so many of the places that I'd visited on my trip through the old Eastern Europe did.

Dubrovnik can be seen to comprise of three main elements: the peninsula of Lapad, where most of the package holiday hotels were located; the strip along the coast where the beaches and rocky bays are to be found; and the *pièce de résistance*, the stunning walled Old Town.

As is my tradition, the first thing I wanted to do in a new place was to see it from on high. And I felt it was fitting too that the first thing I had done when I had landed in Lithuania was take the cable-car up Zaliakalnis Hill to the Church of the Resurrection and now one of the last, over 2,000 kilometres later, would be to take another cable-car up another hill to look down on the beautiful Old Town of Dubrovnik.

Located just north of the city walls, nestled amongst houses and holiday lets, is the cable car station on *Petra Kresimira* which whisks you 400 metres up to the top of Mount Srđ for some truly spectacular views over the terracotta-tiled rooftops of the Old Town and out over the island of Lokrum into the shimmering beauty of the Adriatic. From here you can see just how stunning the scenery is, the perfectly walled-in Old Town perched on an outcrop from the coastline, facing magnificently out to sea. The views are stunning, up the coast, over the city and out towards the islands filling the horizon.

Dubrovnik, despite being even at that time a well-established tourist hot-spot and a World Heritage site, was not immune from the conflict that raged through the Balkans in the early 1990s. From October 1991 until May of 1992, a period of seven months, the town was attacked with artillery fire by the Yugoslav People's Army (the JNA) mainly comprised of Serbian and Montenegrin fighters. The historic Old Town and city walls were attacked, and many buildings were shelled and dozens killed.

As with Sarajevo and Mostar, I can remember watching the TV news images of the shelling of the city walls and recoiling at the senselessness of it all. Reconstruction work carefully repaired the damage, with original buildings restored in line with UNESCO guidelines, all within four years of the end of the war and coincided, in 1999, with the opening of the cable car. From the top, you can see that some of the roofs below have slightly different shades and textures of tiles, but other than that, unless you knew the history, it would not be obvious that this beautiful place had recently been a war zone. At the summit, along with the ubiquitous restaurants and gift shops, there is also a small museum which documents the defence of the city and is well worth taking some time out to visit.

Following tourists around the Old Town

Back down from the cable car, the Old Town beckoned. The heat of the day and the size of the crowds were not going to make this a relaxing stroll but the beauty was unmistakable regardless. The trick would be to avoid the endless processions of tour parties, mostly straight off a cruise liner and being escorted around the town for the afternoon, before being transported back to the ship with their souvenirs and memories. So I chose to start with a hike, up and along the magnificent city ramparts.

Walking around the city walls is a 'must do' part of the Dubrovnik experience. Key details according to my tourist pamphlet – 25 metres high above the streets and alleys below, with sixteen towers and a fortress built-in, the walk right the way around the city walls is nearly 2 kilometres in length. The views over the sea and coves, and of the buildings and squares of the town below, are sensational. Even the interminable struggle to elbow your way to the best vantage points on the ramparts and avoid accidentally photo-bombing posed shots is worth it for the experience of seeing this beautiful old town from these imposing city walls.

The outermost part of the walk, facing out to sea, is the busiest in terms of tourists, for two reasons. Firstly, there are a couple of small cafes and watering holes that afford respite from the heat and the welcome relief of being able to grab more water to hydrate. The heat in Croatia, whilst less intense than in Bosnia, was still fierce with the sun beating down without much shade to lessen the rays. The other reason is that it provides a vantage point from which to watch locals – and, no doubt, hardy tourists and travellers – take the plunge off a rocky ledge beneath the walls and into the blue waters of the Adriatic below.

There are three entry/exit points for the walls: at the main entrance to the Old Town from the Pile Gate; at the north-east entrance via the Ploce Gate next to *Sveti Luka* fortress; and half-way round the walk at the promontory between the sea and the enclosed port, at the *Sveti Ivan* fortress. Many people seemed to take this latter option and head back down into the cooler, shaded back streets of the Old Town but I was intent on completing the full circuit, though I admit a welcome rest was taken on a stone ledge that looked out over the old port where pleasure boats shuttled backwards and forwards taking tourists out to the islands and round the bay.

The last leg, along the northern walls, is where the steepest climbs are to be found, but this section also affords the most spectacular views over the streets and buildings of the Old Town below. It also showcases all the little bars and restaurants that populate the narrow alleys that run north from the main thoroughfare, and which – on a day as hot as today – were motivating me to pay them a visit.

Circuit complete, descending down the steep stone stairs takes you out onto the main 'street' in the Old Town, called the *Stradun*. As this is next to the main entrance from the west at Pile Gate where the vast majority of visitors first set foot into the Old Town, it is the busiest thoroughfare in the town. Populated by designer outlets, souvenir shops and a preponderance of cafes and ice cream parlours, it is a great place to first soak up the atmosphere of Dubrovnik, with throngs of tourists and cruise line day visitors milling around the surprisingly slippery stoned street and walking deeper into the Old Town.

At the end of the *Stradun* the street opens out to the right onto Luža Square, where some of the most beautiful buildings are located. On the left is the sixteenth century Sponza Palace, also known as the *Divona*, meaning 'customs', in a nod to its previous usage as the Customs House, with its inner courtyard and mix of Gothic and Renaissance architecture. Next to the palace is the fifteenth century clock tower, which can be seen the length of the *Stradun*; at 30 metres high it is one of the most famous and most photographed landmarks of the Old Town. In the middle of the square stands Orlando's Column, a stone pillar with the embedded carving of an ancient knight, topped by a small precariously situated platform used traditionally for public proclamations. The column is a popular meeting place for locals and visitors alike.

Dominating the square is the Baroque beauty of *Crkva Svetog Vlaha* (St Blaise's Church), named after the patron saint of Dubrovnik. With its wide staircase and terrace leading up to the entrance it is a popular place to sit in the shade and watch the world pass by.

Continuing south behind St Blaise's takes you along *Ulica Pred Dvorom* to another cluster of magnificent buildings. On the left stands *Knežev Dvor*, the Rector's Palace, a stunning thirteenth century Venetian-Gothic building replete with a six-colonnade entrance which today houses both the city hall and a concert hall. And next to that, the imposing *Katedrala Velike Gospe*, Dubrovnik's Cathedral of the Assumption of the Virgin, its façade flanked by four giant Corinthian columns. A church has stood on this site since the seventh century, with one iteration rumoured to have been part-financed by Richard the Lionheart after he was shipwrecked off the coast when returning from the Crusades. Since being rebuilt after a huge earthquake in 1667, the cathedral has subsequently withstood both another earthquake (in 1979) and shelling during the Siege of Dubrovnik in 1991, though thankfully the damage has been repaired and the building restored to its former glory.

From here, you can take a brief walk out of the Old Town through the *Vrata od Ribarnice* (Fishmarket Gate) to the cobbled terrace overlooking the old port, where you can find various bars and restaurants to grab some food and take the weight off your feet. Beware though, Dubrovnik is not cheap. It was a bit of a culture shock to me, after so long in the old more remote Eastern Europe – I think I spent more money in Dubrovnik in a day or two than I had in the previous weeks in Bosnia, Serbia or Ukraine! Still, the views are lovely, the seafood delicious and the cold drinks especially welcome.

Suitably refreshed, the remainder of my ambling through the Old Town of Dubrovnik was much more peaceful. Away from the tourist routes, the Old Town is a maze of narrow alleys and hidden squares, some admittedly still busy with bars and restaurants on all sides, but some hidden gems are to be found too. The narrow streets leading northwards off the *Stradum* are particularly appealing, with the seating from little bars and bistros winding their way up the cobbled paths. If you time it right (early morning or late afternoon/evening) strolling around Dubrovnik's Old Town can be blissful. One word of warning though. When I did this trip, the crowds were plentiful, but manageable. Since then though, the worldwide phenomenon that is 'Game of Thrones' has hit TV screens and ignited a fan base of millions, and since it is partly filmed in Dubrovnik, the little streets and squares of the Old Town are now awash with 'Thronies' all jostling for photo opportunities at the sites of their fictional heroes, and shops are now bedecked with memorabilia. Not that that should put you off visiting such a beautiful place, but it is wise to be pre-warned!

With most of the tourist crowds gone, and the cruise liner groups long since ferried back to their ships, the evening ambience in Dubrovnik was much more rewarding. I found a little restaurant on a quiet square, ordered a nice seafood paella and a few glasses of chilled *Karlovačko* beer and sat as the sun began to set and thought back over my epic journey now that it was all but at an end. In a day or so, I'd be at the airport and checking in to fly home to Scotland, but the memories of my voyage from the Baltic to the Balkans would stay with me for ever. It seemed almost inconceivable to me that my journey was ending, but it had reinforced in me the love of travel, the desire to see parts of the world that are perhaps not necessarily obvious destinations but which have so much to offer in their history, their people and their cultures.

Finally...the sea!

I had promised myself, through all my travels on overnight trains and amidst uncommon heatwaves, that when I finally made it to the coast then I would hit the water.

With a few hours to kill before I had to make it to the airport, I set off the next morning to see the Lapad peninsula to the west of Dubrovnik where most of the package holiday hotels are located. I'd been told that the No.6 bus ran frequently from outside the Pile Gate at the west of the Old Town and that it would take me on a circular route around Lapad and back. I got off at *Ulica Kralja Tomislava* where a lot of the bars and restaurants seemed to be, and walked down a tree-lined lane towards the water. Though there are no doubt better beaches and swimming spots to be found in Dubrovnik (to the east of the Old Town and on the steep coastal strip west towards Lapad) I didn't have the luxury of time and this spot would do me just fine. With beachfront bars behind me and hotels rising up on the green hills to either side of me, this little horseshoed bay with its pebbled beach would be the final stop on my journey.

Swimming in the sea is such a treat, with the gentle waves and the saltiness of the water beating the artificialness of a swimming pool for me anytime, and as I bobbed about it struck me that this was the first time in many years that I'd actually swum in the sea. The holidays I'd had in my late twenties and early thirties, in Italy or France or the Algarve, had frequently included trips to the beach but since my divorce and my reincarnation as a traveller to more remote parts of the world, it was a pleasure that had not been so readily available to me. And so I treasured the moment, a last memory from a trip abounding with memories, as I thought of the roads and miles that lay behind me, the people I'd met, the countries, cities and towns I'd visited, and the cultures and history I'd experienced.

Not a normal holiday, but one that had surpassed all my expectations. I had a lot to thank Michael Palin for.

The beautiful walled Old Town of Dubrovnik, from Srđ Hill

Rector's Palace and City Hall (top left); Old Town from City Walls (bottom left); and Dubrovnik Old Town's main thoroughfare, the Stradum (right)

EPILOGUE

I wrote this book for a number of reasons.

Partly due to my love of travel, and because a number of people over the years had told me I should commit my experiences to print (though it may just have been that they wanted me to shut up about my travels, and telling me to go away and write a book was an easy escape for them!).

Partly also because I had always been envious of anyone who could be so creative as to produce something that anyone else would want to experience – a song, a novel, a painting, or a portfolio of photographs. Anything that would stir an emotion, something that would leave a legacy.

Back to my friend Alan, for a moment. Whilst I was in the middle of writing this book, we were travelling down to the north-east of England to see friends and to watch a football match and the subject of legacy came up. A relative of his had been working on the new Queensferry Crossing, the newest bridge across the River Forth connecting Edinburgh and the Lothians with Fife to the north. Alan's view was that his relative would be able, with great pride, to say in later life: 'I helped build that bridge'. And what a commendable legacy that would be. Alan's observation – as someone who works in Risk Management for a retail bank – was that if his daughter or even granddaughter asked him in later life, 'Daddy, what did you do for a living?' his only answer would be to say 'I went to a lot of meetings'. Which, for me, summed exactly why I wanted to write this book. I'd spent twenty years marketing credit cards, insurance products and legal services. I wasn't an engineer. A singer-songwriter. A poet. An architect. I didn't really have anything I could point to and say 'I created that'. But I wanted to be able to do so, and the only way I knew how was to document my passion for travel and hope that someone, somewhere, at some point would pick it up and enjoy reading about an excursion from the Baltic Sea to the Balkan coast, through countries long-hidden from the world but which convey such beauty and fascination. And in the worst case scenario that any literary agent or prospective publisher thought it a waste of a tree, then at least I would have a copy on my own bookshelf and be able to point to it and say 'I wrote that'.

And there was also a part of me (the part of me with the ego) that wanted to produce something that might perhaps inspire others. To encourage people to follow their dreams, to dare to go out and experience what had captured their imagination as a small child in the way that watching these aforementioned holiday programmes on dark winter nights in the 1970s and reading travel supplements from weighty Sunday newspapers had instilled in me a desire to see as much of the world as I possibly could.

And so, that would be my message to anyone who has read this far. Do not be afraid. Do not put off until tomorrow what you could do today. The world is a huge and beautiful place. But equally it is small and interconnected where travel is concerned, and getting to places – as I did, for instance, with the Lviv I first witnessed via Michael Palin – is so much easier now than it has ever been. The much-maligned low-cost airlines fly to (or at least pretty near to) places on your bucket-list, I guarantee. Trains will help you cross countries and continents. Buses will take you places where the trains don't. And almost everywhere, so long as you are polite and make an effort, people will be unceasingly helpful and friendly and point you in the direction of where you want to go. If you have ever wanted to go and visit Nepal, South America, North Africa or take a train journey 2,000 kilometres down through the countries of the old Eastern Europe, then do it. You won't regret it.

And if you are worried or think it is too far outside your comfort zone, let me tell you a secret. I have travelled, alone, across South America (twice!) from the remote wilderness of Patagonia to the lunar-like landscapes of the Atacama Desert. I have journeyed around South East Asia, through Cambodia, Vietnam and Laos on tuk-tuks and rickety old buses. I made my way from the Baltic coast down through the beautiful, historic countries of the old Central and Eastern Europe to the Balkan coast. I love travelling. I love it enough to write a book on it and bore people at parties. But I also suffer from homesickness. At times when I am away, I am counting the number of days until I am home again, in my own surroundings, in my own bed. Even though I love every moment of my travel experiences, there is part of me that doesn't want to be there. It might be more than homesickness – it might also be a degree of loneliness, being so far away from home all alone. It may also sometimes be a lack of self-confidence, which may seem strange given that I've successfully managed to negotiate my way around various continents pretty much on my own. It is the strangest dichotomy, but one which I have learned to live with and embrace. So if there is something you've always wanted to do, but are worried that you'll not be able to cope for whatever reason, then rest assured that you are not alone. And if I can overcome my worries, and experience the history and culture and beauty of so many places, then I am confident that you can too.

Wherever it is that takes your fancy, whatever the answer is to your own 'where have you always wanted to go?' question, I would urge you to seize the opportunity and go and experience it. And if it is the lure of the old Eastern Europe – the fortitude of Baltic states like Lithuania; the frontier lands of Ukraine; the history embedded in the old Austro-Hungarian Empire; the turbulent past but vibrant present of the Balkan states, from the exuberance of Belgrade to the cosmopolitan Sarajevo – then I hope this book has been of interest to you, and in some small way, has inspired you in the way that Michael Palin inspired me all those years ago.

Thank you for reading, and *bon voyage*.